WILLIAM AND MARY MEN'S SOCCER

Al Albert

Albert-Daly Field is packed to capacity for a 2004 match in which the Tribe upset then-number-one-ranked Maryland 1-0. The goal was scored on a header by Brannon Thomas, who had returned late in the previous season from brain surgery. Thomas won the Colonial Athletic Association's (CAA) John Randolph Inspiration Award the same year. (Courtesy of William and Mary Library Archives.)

FRONT COVER: Wade Barrett, cocaptain and All-American in 1997, is shown as a senior for the Tribe. Wade went on to an extremely successful and steady career in Major League Soccer (MLS). He was twice captain of the MLS champion Houston Dynamo. Barrett came to W&M from nearby Beach FC (Virginia Beach Travel Soccer, Inc.) soccer club. (Courtesy of William and Mary Library Archives.)

COVER BACKGROUND: Busch Field is packed for the 1994 CAA final between the Tribe and JMU. (Courtesy of William and Mary Sports Information.)

BACK COVER: Mike Flood slots home the winning goal in the final seconds of overtime of the 1983 ECAC South final versus George Mason, earning William and Mary a berth in the NCAA tournament. (Courtesy of William and Mary Sports Information.)

WILLIAM AND MARY MEN'S SOCCER

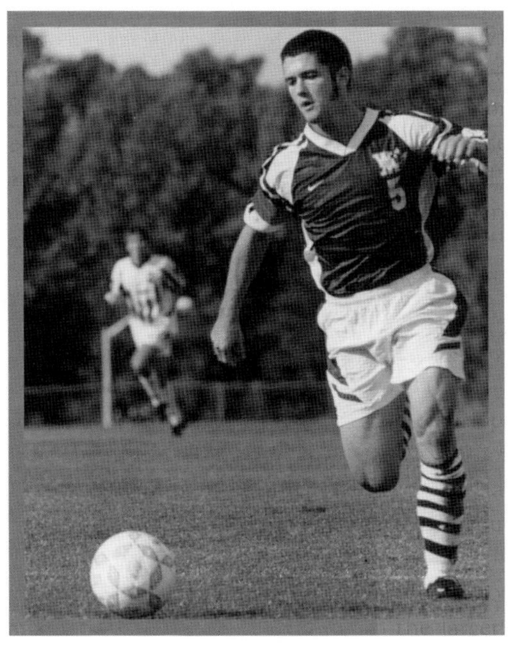

Al Albert
Foreword by Jon Stewart

Copyright © 2010 by Al Albert
ISBN 978-0-7385-6694-8

Published by Arcadia Publishing
Charleston SC, Chicago IL, Portsmouth NH, San Francisco CA

Printed in the United States of America

Library of Congress Control Number: 2009935598

For all general information contact Arcadia Publishing at:
Telephone 843-853-2070
Fax 843-853-0044
E-mail sales@arcadiapublishing.com
For customer service and orders:
Toll-Free 1-888-313-2665

Visit us on the Internet at www.arcadiapublishing.com

This book is dedicated to all those who sweated and sacrificed to make Tribe soccer what it is today—players, coaches, and most notably, my family.

CONTENTS

FOREWORD

When Coach first approached me in the fall of 2009 about an idea he had been working on, I thought . . . how much is this going to cost me? As it turns out, he only wanted my time to contribute a foreword for a book he was writing on Tribe soccer . . . and some money . . . and some signed books for a local auction. But you never mind doing a little something for Coach, because you know he is only doing it for someone else. The story of Tribe soccer really is the story of Coach Albert's dedication and tenacity, creating a tradition and legacy for a program that had no business being as successful as it has ultimately turned out to be. I call the story of Tribe soccer, "Coach Albert: How the Tallest Jew in Southeastern Virginia Made Good."

I first met Coach Albert in 1980 when, as a freshman, I walked into his office to deliver the good news that I, an all-state soccer player (honorable mention) from a powerful program in New Jersey (group two, small, but a class above experimental and home schools) had decided to grace the college soccer program with my presence. The program at that time was at a turning point. The Virginia State Champ plaques and All-American accolades that decorated the walls said big-time program in the making. The pile of green mesh bags filled with dirty uniforms that Coach and J. D. would be carting down to the laundry said the program might not be yet considered "elite." It was in this atmosphere that Coach thanked me for my offer and gently explained the team was well stocked and he would be tracking my progress with their vaunted JV program, which turned out to be not so much a program as a sign-up sheet in a Greek kid's dorm room.

Little did we know that in a few months Tribe soccer would be engaged in an epic battle with Alabama A&M for a spot in the Final Four and that I would be holding down the all-important center midfield spot for a junior varsity clash with an impressive team of orderlies from the mental hospital adjacent to JBT [James Blair Terrace]. (The game ended in a draw. The rules at this time not allowing for penalty kicks and the orderlies said they had to go anyway . . . a code red in the flight risk wing . . . whatever that meant.)

That year, the Tribe settled for a record-setting goal scoring performance (27) by John McManus and green "NCAA Regional Champs" hooded sweatshirts. I wanted only one thing at that point in life: to earn one of those damned sweatshirts . . . and to lose my virginity . . . but I assume that is for the foreword of a very different book. True to his word, Coach had kept an eye on my progress and invited me to join the team for spring workouts leading to a spot on the varsity in the fall. It was an opportunity that I never took for granted.

My years with Tribe soccer were the best of my college experience. The runs out to JBT, the indoor tourneys at Blow Gym, the brawls at ODU, the incredible upset of Penn State at Cary Field and of UConn at Storrs, the banter, the camaraderie, the keg parties on Mataoka

Court and the endless van rides . . . that no matter where we went always seemed to end up at a Sizzler in Fredericksburg, where Coach had a deal on soda refills. "Free refills," Coach would say; "Fredericksburg is not on the way to North Carolina," we would say.

The program in the early eighties was a transitional one. We had some talent and some drive but lacked the discipline and the real thoroughbreds that would be the hallmark of the teams that came after us. The positive spin was we were a team with "personality." I believe the more colloquial term is miscreants. But through it all, Coach displayed the otherworldly patience that was his hallmark. ECAC [Eastern College Athletic Conference] championships and NCAA bids coincided with beer runs and check-bouncing scandals. But Coach always believed that beyond all that obnoxiousness were decent players and decent people. He never gave up on us and never gave up on the program. Hopefully both have made him as proud of our accomplishments as we have been of his.

—Jon Stewart '84

ACKNOWLEDGMENTS

As a freshman at the College of William and Mary, I took a soccer class to satisfy my physical education requirement. The instructor was one "Screaming Joe" Agee, who would later become my varsity soccer coach in 1968, the first winning season ever for W&M men's soccer.

The guys who played for W&M back then were not the best players we have had in our program. Like me, they came from physical education classes, were dropouts from the football team, or just former high school players looking for another chance to play the game. None were recruited, they received very little attention from the school or community, and the only thing motivating them was a true love of the game and the desire to be part of a team.

Years later, we have our own soccer stadium with a practice field, locker room, scholarships, and full-time coaches—everything that a team needs to be successful in Division I soccer today. We hope most of the players still play for the love of the game and team camaraderie.

No doubt my selection of images and the obvious inability to include all of the individuals and teams that played at W&M throughout the years will cause a rash of invectives to be hurled my way by former players who love to repay me for all the grief I gave them during their years as team members. It was tough to decide which pictures would be chosen.

Thanks go to the excellent media relations staff at W&M: Pete Clawson, Kris Sears, Rob Turner, Jacob Skipper, Julia Martin, and Scott Burns. Amy Schindler and her staff at Swem Library were integral to my research. Nat Baako, a feisty central midfielder, was a first-class scanner as well, as was Mallory Shurtz. Terry Driscoll and Bobby Dwyer of W&M Athletics allowed me time away from my Tribe Club duties to complete this project. Peggy Lukas and Jean Beall of the Tribe Club were invaluable proofreaders. Jon "Leibo" Stewart took time from his incredibly busy schedule to write this foreword, and he continues to be the funniest guy in the locker room. Unless otherwise noted, all images are from the William and Mary Library Archives and the William and Mary Sports Information Department.

As always, my most valuable copy editor and syntax expert was my wife, Gail.

INTRODUCTION

In 2008, W&M lost in the second round of the NCAA tournament to a Wake Forest team that was seeded number one in the country. The game was very evenly played and decided by a golden goal in overtime. The Tribe once again demonstrated its capacity to compete against any intercollegiate squad. It had taken many years for the program to get to this level.

The College of William and Mary was founded in 1693 and is the second oldest college in the United States, preceded only by Harvard University. The school has been termed a "Public Ivy," with rigorous admission standards and even more demanding academic course work. Varsity athletes are given little special treatment at W&M; there are no athletic dormitories and no preferential registration for classes.

Despite the rigorous admissions requirements and a limited recruitment pool, the College does manage to compete very adequately in most sports. Typical entering students at W&M are in the top 10 percent of their high school graduating class and in the top decile in standardized testing. Some special consideration is given each year to recruits for men's soccer, but the bottom line is that every student-athlete has to spend 20–30 hours a week playing soccer in addition to satisfying the demands of their course load. The school is also relatively small for a Division 1 competitor, with only about 6,000 undergraduates. Quite often, a random high school player and his parents will drop by the men's soccer office and start the conversation by asking if the school plays in Division I or Division III.

For 45 years, W&M has been a major stimulus for the growth of soccer in southern Virginia. W&M had the first school-sponsored varsity team in the area in the late 1960s, and much of the emergence of youth and high school soccer in the region can be attributed to the school's influence.

From humble beginnings on an off-campus open, grassy area, the program now plays at well-groomed Albert-Daly Field. In the planning is a stadium with amenities that will ensure a great college soccer experience for players and spectators. The players have gone from individuals having no experience other than physical education soccer classes to some of the most highly recruited youth and high school players in the country.

W&M's rise to national prominence in soccer has not been handed to them. Originally, team uniforms were hand-me-down football jerseys and physical education uniforms. Even in 1980, when the team received its first invitation to the NCAA tournament, one rival coach with a large budget was reputed to moan that W&M did not deserve the at-large bid since their program had torn uniforms and could not even afford to replace them. By 1990, the team had one of the first-ever Nike contracts, and from then on, those comments disappeared.

Scholarships were also slow to come. It took 30 years for W&M men's soccer to be fully funded; prior to 1975, there was no athletically related aid for soccer for the team. In 1980, when the team went to the NCAA quarterfinals, the program was meagerly funded at the level of two full scholarships split into partial grants among a number of players. Several starters on that squad never received any soccer scholarship money during their careers. Not until the late 1990s was the team fully funded in grant-in-aids, and then only if it was able to maintain a high percentage of in-state players. In most cases, other regional soccer powers were well funded much earlier in the development of their programs.

W&M soccer has become a huge extended family with semi-annual reunions and a network of contacts throughout the United States and globally. The 12th Man Club, a division of the Tribe Club that raises money specifically for men's soccer, has raised almost a million dollars for the program over the past 20 years from alumni, parents, and supporters. An international trip every four years has become a big part of each player's experience. Since the first trip in 1976, the team has twice been to England, Jamaica, Bermuda, and Greece.

Al Albert, the author of this book, was the coach of the W&M men's team for 33 years from 1971 to 2003 and is one of only five individuals to ever head the men's varsity soccer program. He also played for W&M in the 1960s. Over 350 men have played at W&M, including a number who have gone on to professional careers and international competition. Many W&M alumni and former assistant coaches have also gone on to careers in youth, high school, and college coaching.

In short, the W&M men's soccer program represents much more than a tradition of winning seasons and championships. It is most proudly represented by the way in which it has influenced the growth of soccer in southeastern Virginia and by the group of individuals that call themselves the members of the "Tribe Soccer Family." The sign over the door as you leave the locker room says it all: "Our Family Versus Their Team."

Compiled through extensive research in school publications, archives, and personal collections, the images selected for this book capture the essence of W&M men's soccer through the past half-century.

Key facts about Tribe men's soccer:

1) Of the 13 opportunities the team has had to compete in the NCAA postseason soccer championship, it has never been eliminated from the tournament by more than one goal. On five occasions, that last loss in the NCAA tournament was in overtime.

2) Tribe soccer strung together 30 straight winning seasons from 1975 to 2004, ranking sixth among all men's Division I soccer programs. Only powerhouses UCLA, Clemson, St. Louis, Indiana, and SMU have longer streaks and only one other (UVA) could possibly pass W&M in the next decade.

3) Twice the Tribe has advanced to the Elite Eight of the NCAA tournament. In 1980, it lost to eventual runner-up Alabama A&M in the 90th minute of regulation, and in 1996, it lost in overtime to St. John's, who went on to win the title.

1

Club Soccer to Varsity

Soccer in Virginia was not widely played in 1965, the year that W&M first listed a club soccer team in the college yearbook. Only a handful of colleges in the state fielded varsity teams.

Although there was only a club team at W&M that year, the first varsity squad was sanctioned in 1966, during a period in which a number of sports were added. Since no full-time physical education faculty members were well versed in the sport, graduate student Paul McLaughlin was named the first varsity soccer coach in school history. Success was not to come quickly, as the team posted a perfect 0-9 record.

By 1966, home games were played away from the main campus on a grassy area that was never designed as an athletic facility. James Blair Terrace, next to Eastern State Hospital, is today the site of the W&M baseball facility, Plumeri Park. There was a lot of room, but the surface was bumpy, and to make matters worse, the Lions Club Jamboree—a traveling carnival—took place on the site in August, before the soccer season. It was not unusual for the team to have to pick up broken glass, ticket stubs, and other residue from the carnival.

At that time, there was no road between the hospital and the field, and it was common for patients from the mental hospital to visit the team during practices and games. Some would even walk across the field during matches to the amazement of visiting teams and referees, but the W&M players remained unfazed.

When McLaughlin left school after the 1966 season, athletic director Les Hooker considered dropping the sport. According to legendary W&M coaching icon Joe Agee, who had been teaching soccer in physical education, it was a critical moment for the program. Agee agreed to coach the team in 1967, although his knowledge of the game was also limited.

Despite his self-admitted lack of soccer expertise, Agee coached the team for two years, and in 1968, he managed to lead the team to its first-ever winning season with a 5-4-1 record, including an upset at home over a strong Roanoke College squad. That team included a strong sophomore class that would two years later produce the first outstanding record at W&M. The *Colonial Echo* wrote, "You have to wonder if this [men's soccer] will remain a 'minor' sport much longer."

The original team in 1965 poses for a yearbook shot at practice. This picture was taken at the college intramural field, and the team is wearing its physical education uniform apparel. The club was 1-7 with a mixture of international students and former high school players.

Colonial Eleven Triumphs In W&M Soccer Debut

William and Mary's Homecoming weekend, featuring three contests with George Washington, began on a wet losing note — a 10-1 loss to the Colonial soccer team.

Playing in the first inter-collegiate soccer match held on the Reservation, the Indians could never muster a sustained offensive or set a disciplined defense, and the better-equipped Colonials never trailed in the contest.

The crowd watching saw the Indians lose possession and field position numerous times, due primarily to poor footing.

The game, played on the boys' intramural field, consisted of four 22-minute quarters. George Washington scored in every quarter, leading 2-0 at the end of the first period.

This lead was increased to 4-0 in the second quarter, before Pete Clarke, captain of the team, drilled home a one-pointer mid-way in the period to make the score 4-1.

Leading 6-1 going into the third quarter, GW added two more points in that period, and two more in the final frame.

Though William and Mary had conducted but few practices before this first game and the number of experienced players is few, the score is not a true indication of the game.

At least four times the Indians moved the ball down the field well only to lose it by over-running the ball.

The defense, too, suffered because of the conditions. Many times, the Tribe could not stop and start fast enough to keep up with the disciplined Colonials.

The Tribe is playing with a team of from 15 to 20 players (11 men compose one team), including four from England— Brian Clarke, Guy Temple, Martin Burrough, and Mike King-Harran — and one with many years of soccer experience in South America — captain Pete Clarke.

CLARK ADVANCES BALL

Brian Clark makes valiant effort against GW in 10-1 loss. Ref Tom Chapman (former Vermont State star) readies whistle.

According to this October 29, 1965, issue of the *Flat Hat*, W&M's student newspaper, the first soccer game ever played on campus was a loss to George Washington on the W&M intramural field. It was played on homecoming weekend, and the article cites the poor field conditions.

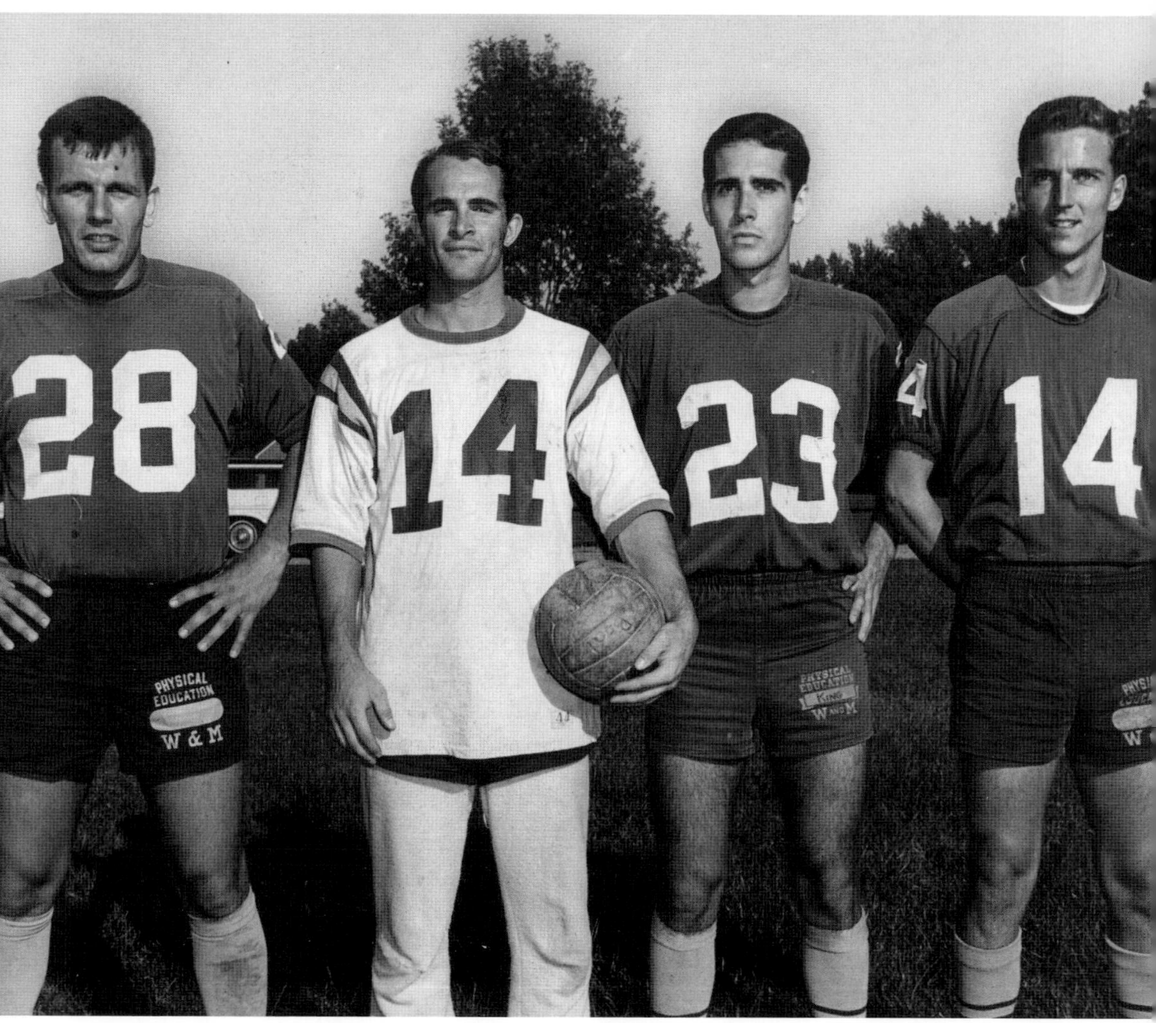

These are publicity pictures for some of the members of the 1966 team: (from left to right) Bill Smith, Art Louise, Gary King, and Pete Clarke. The players were lined up in the photo shoot to save film, and there were four on each print. That year's uniform consisted of old football jerseys; Louise's is white because he was the goalkeeper. He had been a defensive back on the football team in prior years. The 18-panel leather ball was probably twice the weight of today's balls. The team shorts were the physical education shorts that all freshmen and sophomores were required to buy and wear in activity classes. Louise and Smith were athletes who left the football team and were looking for some competition, as was teammate Dale Mueller. King made All–Southern Conference that year as a fullback—the first player in school history to be recognized on any all-star soccer squad.

SOCCER

Shoes	$150.00
Sweatsuits	130.00
Travel (6 games)	600.00
Officials (6 home games)	360.00
Visiting teams (6 games)	400.00
Recruiting	50.00
Letter Awards	100.00
Publicity	50.00
VISA Dues	25.00
ISFAA Dues	25.00
NCSA Dues	10.00
Tape and Medical Expenses	150.00
Insurance	600.00
	$2650.00

Scorebook
Pins

This budget document from one of the first seasons is bare bones, even if adjusted for inflation. It is interesting that the cost of insurance is in the team budget and, along with travel, is the most expensive line item. Recruiting and publicity were apparently not priorities, and laundry pins and a scorebook were not funded at all. The annual expenditure for men's soccer now at W&M is about $500,000.

The 1966 team picture is from the *Colonial Echo*, although a number of players are missing: from left to right are (first row) Larry Dillon, Bill Crewe, Larry Foy, John Burleigh, Steve Row, and Pete Schleif; (second row) Keith Bricklemeyer, George Fenigsohn, Steve Gaskins, Bob Boal, Art Louise, and coach Paul McLaughlin. The team is still in its football jerseys and continued its growing pains with a 0-9 record.

Paul McLaughlin, the first coach of a W&M soccer team, shouts instructions during the 1966 season. McLaughlin's primary sport was baseball, but he coached the first varsity season for W&M as a graduate student. He went on to teach and coach baseball at the junior college level in New Jersey.

Mike King-Harmon controls the ball against his Fort Eustis opponent during the 1965 season. King-Harmon was one of a handful of British students who formed the nucleus of the first squads fielded by W&M. The team played military teams during the early years to fill out its schedule.

The 1967 squad poses in its numberless uniforms. Apparently by the time the shipment arrived, the team had no time to send them to the printer. Flanking the team are coach Joe Agee (right) and assistant Gary King. Many of the freshmen on this team would eventually form the nucleus of the undefeated 1970 squad.

Legendary W&M coach Joe Agee coached not only the men's soccer team for two years from 1967 to 1968 but also freshman football and basketball as well as varsity baseball and golf. He stepped in to coach soccer when athletic director Les Hooker considered dropping the sport as a varsity activity because of the lack of a coach.

Pictured above, All-South goalkeeper Dave Fabian makes a diving save. Short on technique but blessed with tremendous quickness and agility, Fabian was the first top W&M keeper. He battled injuries his entire career and is ironically now an orthopedic surgeon in the Boston, Massachusetts, area. Fabian started for four years and was W&M's first-ever All-South selection his senior year. Below, Dave comes out for a ball in a crowd at James Blair Terrace during his freshman year (1967). Along with classmates Ed Hartman, Steve Wilson, Scott McEvoy, Bob Jendron, John Dodds, and Bruce Niles, Fabian was a four-year starter.

The 1968 team picture was taken in Blow Gymnasium by the *Flat Hat*, the school newspaper. Posting a 5-4-1 record under second-year coach Joe Agee, this was the first W&M soccer team to have a winning season. Although two of the games were against the inexperienced SEALs from the Little Creek Naval Amphibious Base, W&M did post an upset of nationally ranked Roanoke College.

Bruce Niles goes into a tackle during the 1968 season as John Dodds looks on. Niles played soccer and baseball at W&M and was a senior winger on the undefeated 1970 team. He then assisted Al Albert during the 1971 season and actually had to take over as head coach for a couple of games that season when Albert was hospitalized with mononucleosis.

Jim Carpenter coached the team in 1969 and 1970. Carpenter was a lacrosse coach who succeeded Joe Agee and led the team to its first and only undefeated regular season in 1970. The team was 9-0-2 after 11 games but lost in both the Virginia State and Southern Conference Championship games.

Terry Vought and John Dodds surround All-American Scott Anderson in 1968 as W&M upsets nationally ranked Roanoke at James Blair Terrace. This was the first win against a ranked opponent in W&M soccer history. In the 1960s and even into the early 1970s, smaller colleges like Roanoke, Lynchburg, and Randolph-Macon were often the strongest teams in the state.

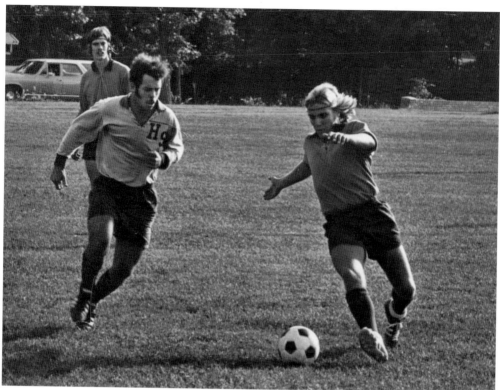

Midfielder Scott McEvoy (1967–1970) dribbles against an unidentified Hampden-Sydney opponent in a 4-0 win in Williamsburg. In the background is midfielder John Dodds. The team has moved on to a modern, 32-panel, black-and-white ball. This game was played at James Blair Terrace, where the W&M baseball stadium, Plumeri Park, stands today.

Dale Mueller plays a ball forward during the 1967 season. In the background, teammates Bob Boal and Ed Hartman watch. Mueller was one of the former football players who switched over to soccer during the 1965–1967 period.

2

First Steps Forward

The 1970 team was the first hugely successful soccer squad at W&M. It finished the regular season 9-0-2 but lost in both the Southern Conference and Virginia State Championship games.

The Tribe had been building toward success for several years, but the catalyst arrived in the form of transfer Phil Essman, who had to sit out the 1969 season. Essman led the team in scoring with 11 goals in 13 games and was subsequently named Virginia College Player of the Year.

At the end of the successful 1970 season, eight senior starters graduated, leaving a huge rebuilding job for new coach Al Albert. Albert replaced Jim Carpenter, whom he had assisted in soccer and lacrosse in the previous season. When Carpenter left for Colorado in June 1971, physical education department chairman Howard Smith offered Albert the job of head coach of both the soccer and lacrosse teams and a full-time physical education position.

Albert's first three seasons were marked by moderate success, but it was not until 1974 that the team finished with another winning record. It would then be 30 years before W&M men's soccer would fail to field a winning team.

In Northern Virginia, the Annandale Boys Club had amassed a youth club team capable of winning a national title. It did just that in 1976 with its Cavaliers under-19 team. The head of the Annandale Boys Club, Everett Germain, became very actively involved in supporting the budding W&M program, and as a result, the school began to give soccer scholarships. Germain's son, Kip, came to W&M along with a number of his club teammates.

By 1977, W&M was winning a lot of games, and from 1978 to 1980, it won the Virginia State College Championship three times, at that time called the VIL (Virginia Intercollegiate League). The 1970s were a period of growth for Tribe soccer, but no one would have predicted the way the 1980 season would unfold.

The undefeated 1970 team is pictured, from left to right, at James Blair Terrace: (first row) John Dodds, Mark Taylor, Bruce Niles, Phil Essman, Dave Fabian, Bob Jendron, Scott McEvoy, Steve Wilson, and Ed Hartman; (second row) Gary Duggan, Dave Oelberg, Tim Stamps, Mike Berbert, Tom McGovern, Mike Wren, and Rich Atkinson; (third row) head coach Jim Carpenter, manager Bob Mathews, Jeff Greim, Clement Brown, Val Stieglitz, B. A. Miller, John Olsen, and assistant coach Al Albert.

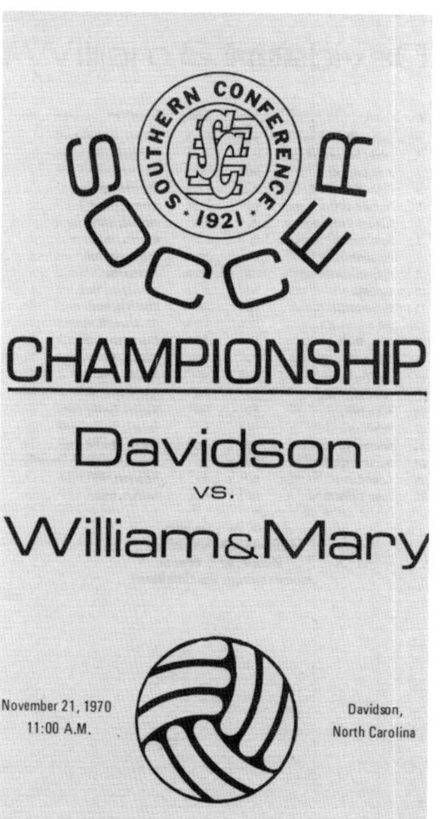

SOUTHERN CONFERENCE
1921
SOCCER
CHAMPIONSHIP
Davidson
vs.
William&Mary
November 21, 1970
11:00 A.M.
Davidson,
North Carolina

This program is from the first championship game in which the Tribe ever played—a Southern Conference match at Davidson. After its unbeaten season, the Tribe lost both the Southern Conference final to Davidson and then the Virginia State final to UVA. The team had eight senior starters and would have to rebuild in 1971.

The 1972 team picture was taken at James Blair Terrace. Despite a 5-7-0 record, the Indians lost a close 1-0 game at league power Appalachian State in the Southern Conference playoffs. The players, from left to right, are (first row) Gary Duggan, Tim Stamps, Boro Djordjevic, Mike Berbert, Dave Oelberg, John Allman, and Jeff Greim; (second row) Gordon Eide, Bruce Cleland, Joe Dunbeck, Joe Cosimano, Art Cone, Gates Parker, Heldur Liivak, and John Olsen; (third row) Bernie Leister, Steve Proscino, Gerry Fitzpatrick, Scott Satterfield, Trevor Smith, Scott MacLaren, Jim Fox, Allen Beasley, Ridge Dewitt, Rick Rheinhart, and coach Al Albert. Jeff Greim (right) was a tri-captain in 1972 along with Mike Berbert and Tim Stamps and was the sole captain in 1973. Scott MacLaren was named to the All-South team.

The September 23 issue of the 1973 *Flat Hat* proclaimed, "Soccer Team Gets Greatest Win." The reference was to the 3-2 sudden-death overtime win over the Campbell Camels in their own classic. Down 2-0 at the half, the Indians stormed back on a second-half goal from Scott Satterfield assisted by Mark Healy and a penalty kick taken by Trevor Smith. In overtime, the defense, anchored by goalkeeper Casey Todd and sweeper Jeff Greim, thwarted the Camel attack. Eight minutes into overtime, Tad Minkler assisted Satterfield on his second goal of the night to seal the win. Todd (below) was named MVP, and midfielders Minkler (second row, second from right above) and Scott MacLaren (third from right) were also named to the tourney all-star squad. W&M finished the season with a 6-5-1 record but was fifth in the Southern Conference.

This picture is from a home game against UVA in 1974 at the intramural field, next to William and Mary Hall. Freshman defender Charlie Hensel is competing for a header against UVA's star forward No. 10, Jay Meaney. Watching the challenge from left to right are W&M defenders Vins Sutlive and Ridge DeWitt. The game ended in a 1-1 tie. Hensel was the first player ever to get athletic scholarship money at W&M, the princely sum of $500 for his freshman year.

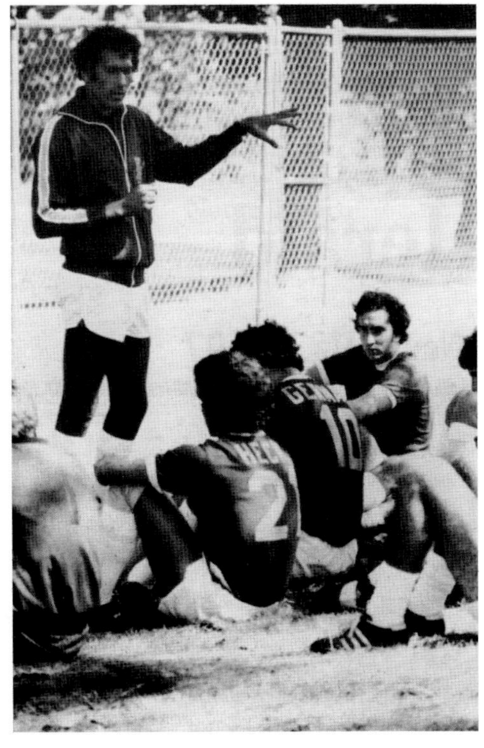

Al Albert lectures his team at halftime during a game in 1975 at the intramural field. By this time, portable speakers were being brought in to announce starting lineups and play music for warm-ups and halftime. The team moved into its present locker facility at brand-new W&M Hall and would soon move to Cary Field. Seated players from left to right are Al Heck, Kip Germain, and Vins Sutlive.

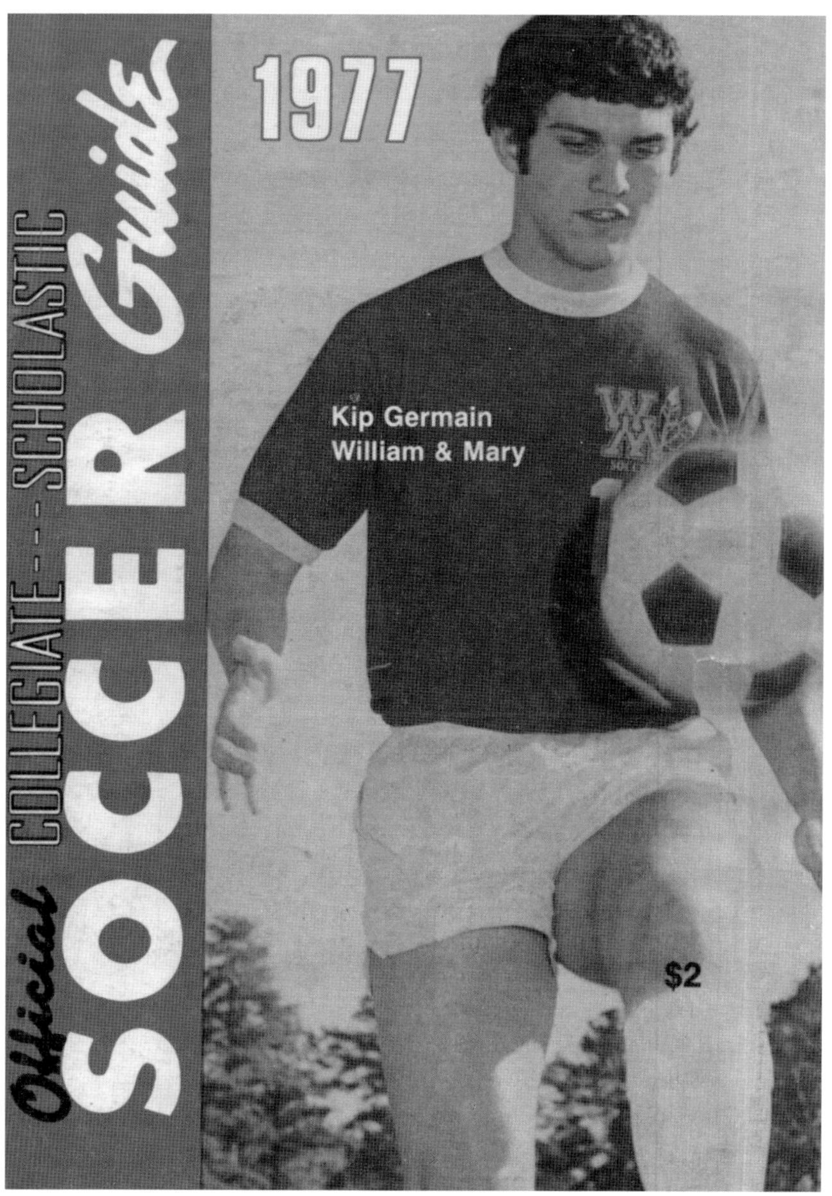

Kip Germain was the biggest recruit to come to W&M in the 1970s. He was the star of the Annandale Cavaliers club team that won the 1976 national under-19 club championship, the McGuire Cup. Other top players from that club team to play for the Tribe were Chris Davin, Eduardo Lopez, Ben Glass, and John Bray. Younger Annandale players such as Rob Olson and Mark Gardiner soon followed. Germain is pictured here juggling on the cover of the *Official Soccer Guide*, at that time the most widely distributed periodical for college and high school soccer. After W&M, Kip played for the Washington Diplomats alongside legendary Johan Cruyff. Despite battling knee injuries, he is seventh all-time in points at W&M and is tied for fifth in goals scored with 36. His 16-goal season in 1976 is the fourth highest season goal total in program history.

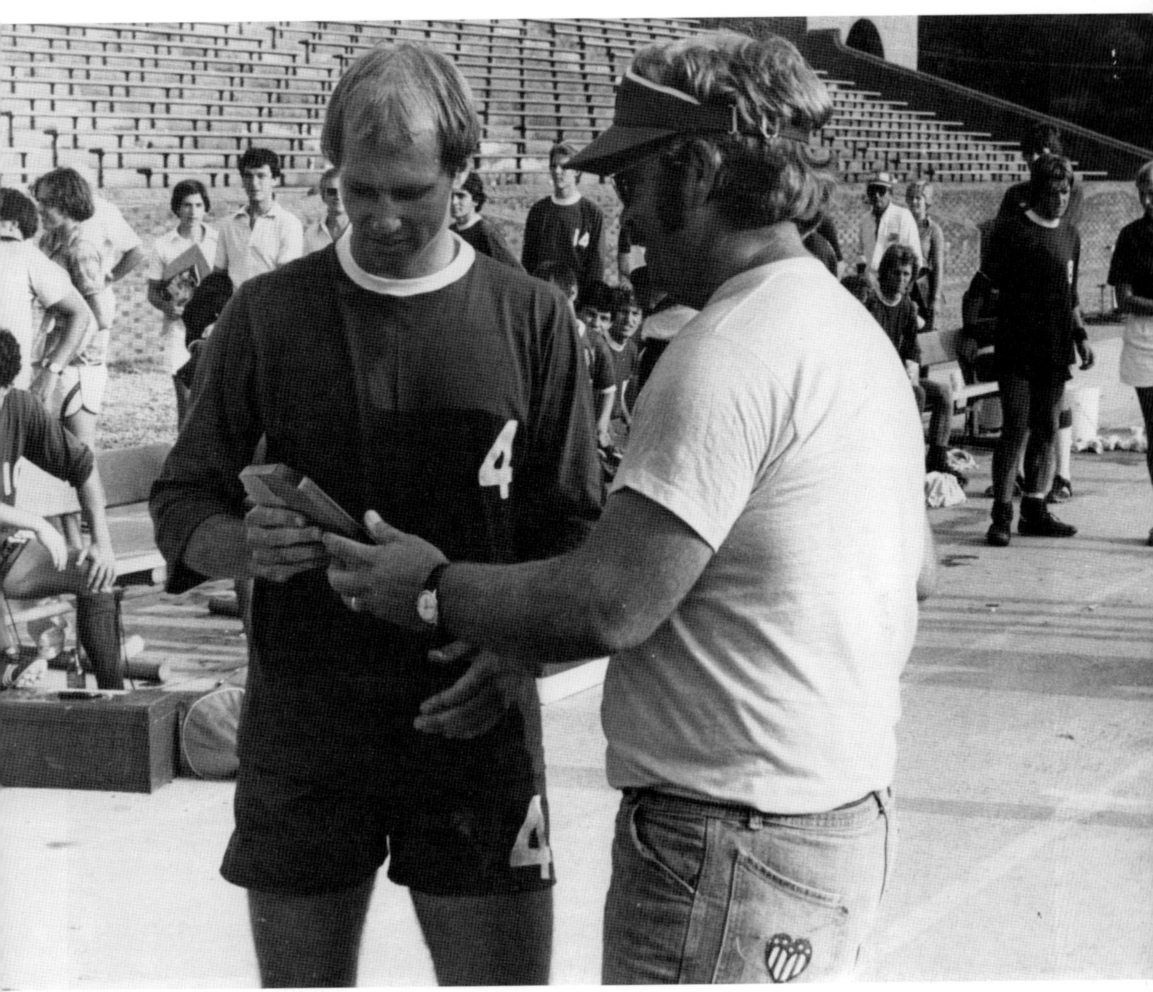

Another star of the mid-1970s at W&M was Bill Watson, seen here accepting an award from Kiwanian Ray Adams at the Williamsburg Kiwanis Soccer Classic at Cary Field. Watson was a top recruit from the St. Andrews Soccer Club in Toronto the same year that Kip Germain came to campus, and he was a three-time All-American in 1975, 1977, and 1978. Watson also played varsity lacrosse and, for one season, was the Tribe football kicker—once splitting the uprights for a 47-yard field goal. He would practice with the soccer team at the intramural field and run to football practice to kick with them for a few minutes. Bill was named W&M Male Athlete of the Year in 1976 and was drafted by Dallas of the North American Soccer League.

The 1975 team came into the Southern Conference Championship game with great expectations, but the team was not ready for a powerful Appalachian State team, which won the game 3-0 in Williamsburg. The team finished with a respectable 9-4-1 record. Freshman Kip Germain led the team in scoring with 13 goals, and Watson made All-American for the first time. Germain and goalkeeper Casey Todd were also named All-South. Shown here, from left to right, are (first row) T. Smith, Dewitt, Satterfield, Sutlive, Fox, Minkler, Todd, and Thomas; (second row) Simonpietri, Bromfield, Germain, Healy, Carlin, Thomas, Balas, and R. Smith; (third row) L. Berbert, Bender, Coach O'Connor, Hensel, Watson, Simonsen, Ellenbogen, Maher, Ahearn, Manager Greenlaw, and Coach Albert.

APPALACHIAN STATE
WILLIAM & MARY
Soccer
SOUTHERN CONFERENCE
1921
Championships
1975
COLLEGE OF WILLIAM & MARY • WILLIAMSBURG, VIRGINIA

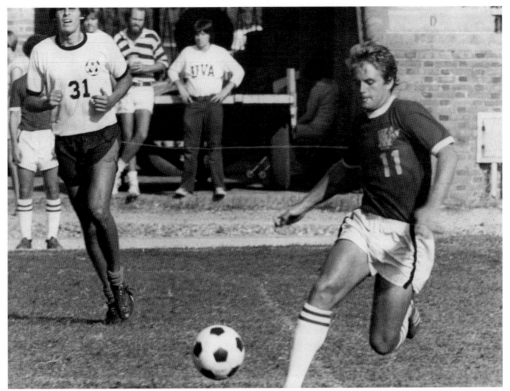

Brad Eure was the first in-state player recruited by W&M from outside the fertile Northern Virginia area. He played for Dave Amsler at Bollingbrook School in Petersburg and was a smart, steady midfield player for the Tribe from 1975 to 1978. He is shown here in games at Cary Field against UVA and Howard. Cary was deemed too narrow for college soccer, and the team would move a decade later to Busch Field, an Astroturf facility behind W&M Hall that was 120-by-75 yards. The soccer surface at Cary was barely 65 yards wide and had a track with a railing around it. It was an intimidating venue for visitors and the scene of some great W&M games, including the 1980 NCAA quarterfinal versus Alabama A&M.

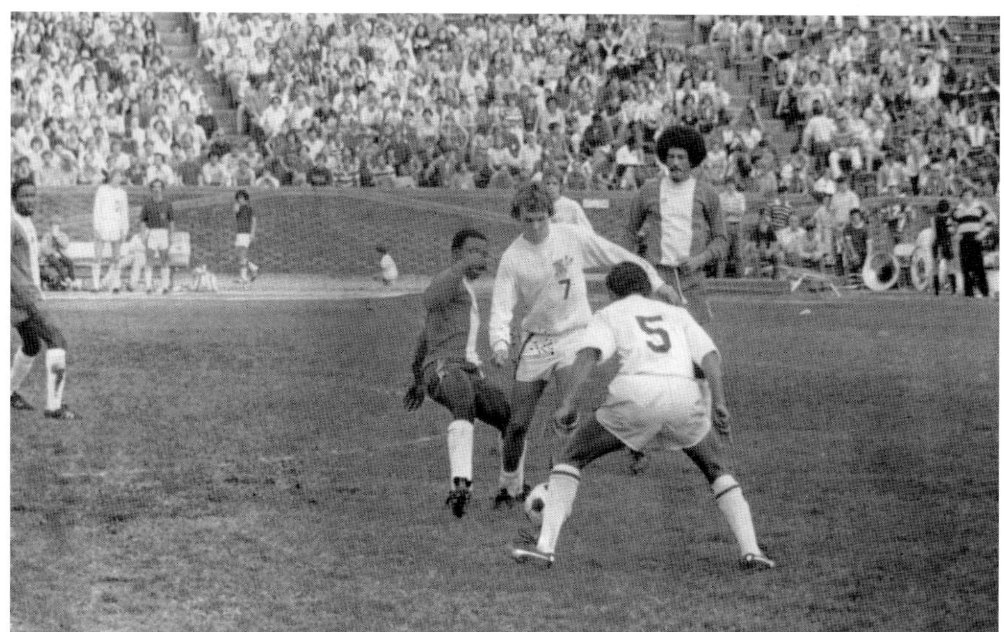

Graham Sykes and Eduardo Lopez battle for control of the midfield against Howard at Cary Field in 1977. On every occasion that W&M met the powerful Bisons in the 1970s, it came up just short. Sykes and Lopez would both be named All-South this season, and the team would finish with a 13-4-0 record.

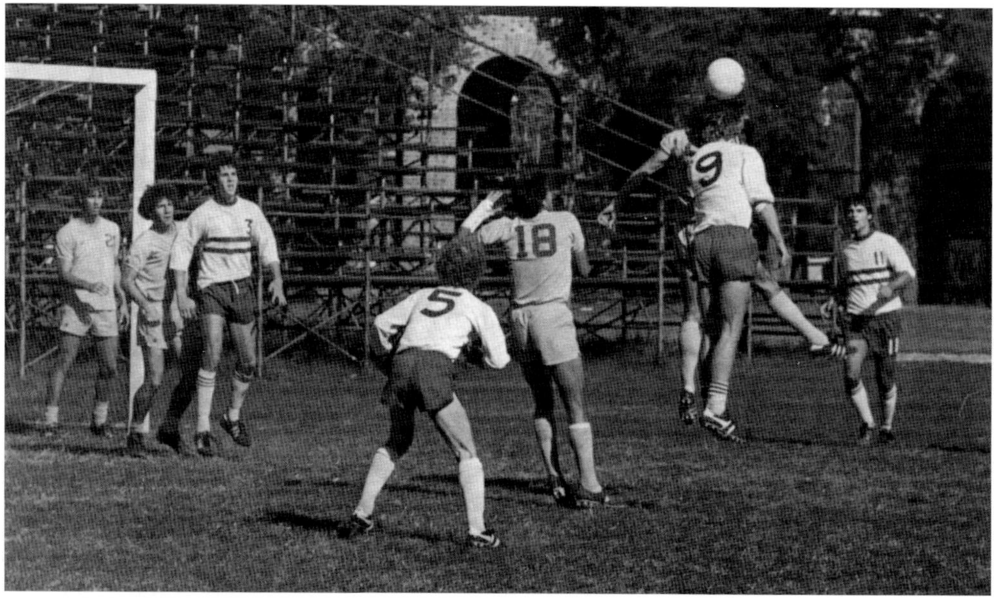

Rob Olson heads a ball to goal in a game at Cary Field in 1979 as Chris Maher, Mike Bedell, and John Chuday look on. Rob was an All-South regional player in 1979 and 1980 and played in the East-West Senior Bowl in 1980. Olson later played for the Georgia Generals in the American Soccer League and Team America, an early version of the U.S. National Team.

Right back John Bray challenges a Randolph-Macon attacker for the ball during the 1976 season. Bray was one of the first players from the national under-19 championship Annandale Cavaliers team to attend W&M. A ferocious defender, he was a standout at his position for four years from 1976 to 1979.

Ben Glass, now an attorney in Northern Virginia, is pictured challenging for the ball on the cover of the 1977 team brochure. Ben was a left back from the Annandale Boys Club who played for the Tribe from 1976 to 1979. He also served as chairman of the 12th Man Club, the fund-raising arm of the soccer team from 1992 to 1996.

Kip Germain scores a goal in a game at Cary Field in 1978. This was the first year of three straight W&M state titles, which gave the team the bragging rights to produce the bumper sticker "W&M Soccer / Best in Virginia." Germain now runs the club his father started, the Annandale Boys and Girls Club.

Chris Davin moves downfield at Cary in a game in 1978. Also in the picture are Steve Graine, Graham Sykes, Bill Watson, Marty Nickley, and Steve Gallop. Davin, from Bishop O'Connell High School in Northern Virginia, was an All-South player in 1979 and was one of the fastest players ever to play for the Tribe.

Three outstanding Canadian players from the late 1970s pose for the camera: (from left to right) Graham Sykes, Steve Gallop, and John McManus. All three came from the Toronto area. Sykes was a talented attacking midfielder who finished his career with 36 goals and made All-South three times. McManus holds the all-time single season scoring record with 27 goals, and Gallop was a four-year starter in goal.

Paul Wise and John McManus look on as a ball is cleared off the line at Cary Field. Wise was the first of three English players who played for the Tribe between 1979 and 1984. He returned to London after two seasons of W&M soccer, and for the past 28 years, he has remained very active in Maccabi soccer in Great Britain. He recently played for the grand masters team, which won the over-45 division in the 18th Maccabiah in Israel.

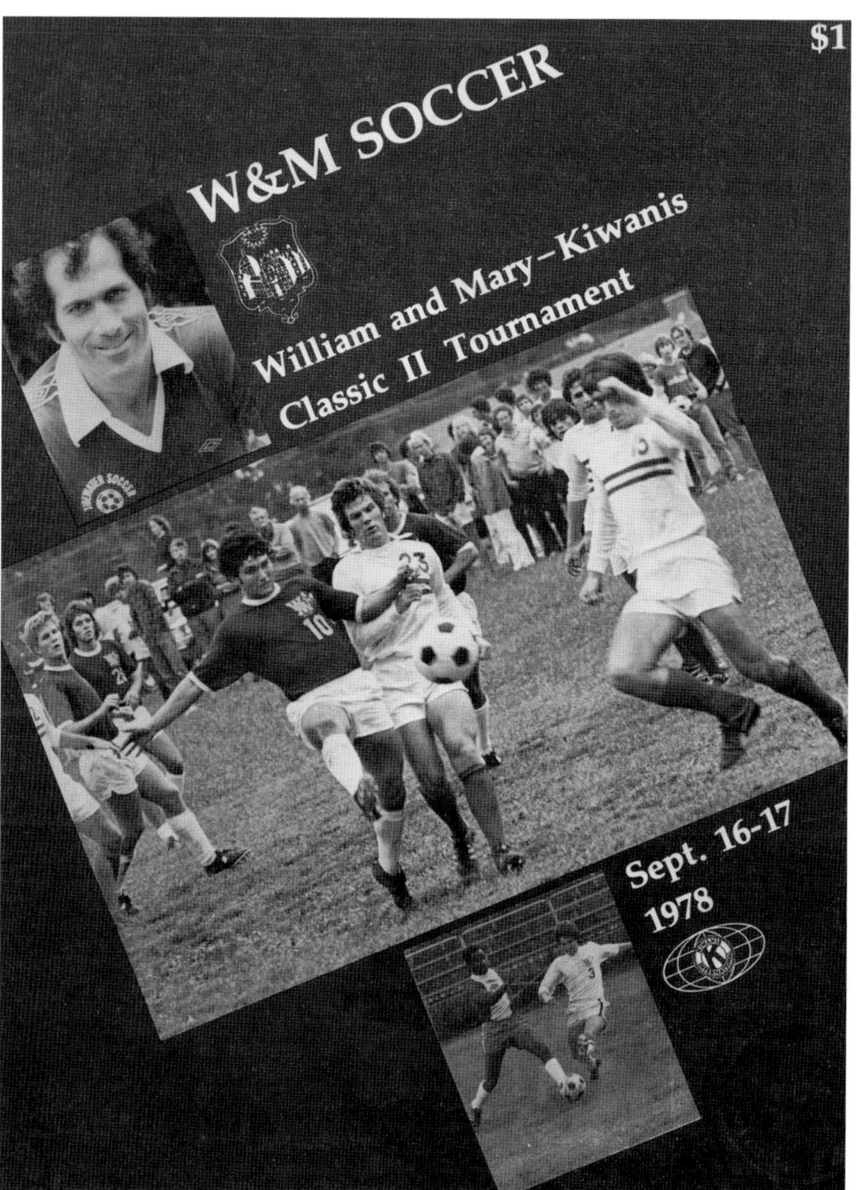

The 1978 yearbook was the first full-size yearbook production by the program. In the center picture, Kip Germain challenges for the ball as Don Pfanz, Graham Sykes, and Bill Watson look on. From 1977 to 1980, the Williamsburg Kiwanis Club sponsored a four-team college tournament in the fall. The tournament program developed into the media guide for the team in subsequent years. The 1978 team won the first of three straight Virginia State titles with a 10-6-3 record, winning in the final over JMU. The team had a terrible 2-5-2 start but then got hot to win not only the Virginia Intercollegiate League (VIL) championship for Division I teams but also the all-college Virginia Intercollegiate Soccer Association (VISA) title with a win over Randolph-Macon. After the season, standouts Germain and Watson were drafted by the North American Soccer League (NASL) teams Washington and Dallas respectively.

3

The Rise of Soccer in Virginia

Prior to the establishment of soccer at W&M in 1965, there were very few high school soccer teams in Virginia and virtually no youth soccer clubs. A decade later, things would change rapidly.

Youth soccer took off in southeastern Virginia in the 1970s. Northern Virginia had an early start with groups such as the Annandale Boys Club, but closer to Williamsburg, the first organizations were in the Peninsula Youth Soccer Association (PYSA), comprised of the Williamsburg Soccer Club, Fort Monroe, and Langley. Soon after, an entry from Virginia Beach joined to make the PYSA a four-club league.

In the area of high school soccer, the private schools had always led the way. By 1975, schools like Lafayette High School in Williamsburg were fielding high school varsity teams for the first time. Northern Virginia had again been a few years ahead in this area, and many of the public schools in Alexandria, Arlington, and Fairfax County had varsity squads.

Camps were a big part of the soccer scene before youth clubs developed comprehensive, year-round programs. The Tidewater Soccer Camp was run by W&M coach Al Albert and was launched in 1974 at Virginia Wesleyan College. It moved two years later to the Williamsburg campus and quickly grew to become one of the largest camps in the area, reaching a height of six weeks and 900 children in 1980.

Among the colleges that had varsity soccer, the power began to shift from the smaller colleges, which had dominated the scene in the 1960s, to the larger universities that would become NCAA Division I. The Virginia Intercollegiate Soccer Association (VISA), which had consisted of schools of all sizes and levels, gave way to the Virginia Intercollegiate League (VIL), which included only Division I teams.

As a state school, this overall growth of soccer in Virginia was a huge factor in W&M's rise to college competitiveness. In the early 1970s, most of the players were from out of state, but by 1996 and the quarterfinal run in the NCAA tournament, most of the starters were Virginia residents.

These are group photographs from the very first Tidewater Soccer Camp in 1974 taken inside the cafeteria at Virginia Wesleyan College, where the camp was held for its first three years. In the first year, before club soccer exploded in southeastern Virginia, the camp had less than 100 overnight campers for the single session. By 1980, there were six consecutive weeks on campus in Williamsburg averaging 150 campers a week. Besides the W&M coaches, the staff usually consisted of present and former players; college coaches from other schools; and international coaches from England, Sweden, Ghana, and Colombia. At present, coach Chris Norris runs one week on campus branded as the Colonial Kicks Soccer Camp. The Tidewater Soccer Camp continues only as a day camp provider.

The first camp staff ever at the Tidewater Soccer Camp included several W&M players (Tom Daskaloff, Joe Carlin, Tad Minkler, and Casey Todd) plus Richmond-area coaches Helmut Werner and Dave Amsler. Others who have worked at Tidewater through the years include former U.S. Soccer head coach Hank Steinbrecher, English pros Richie Norman and Frank Upton, and Football Association staff coach Dick Bate.

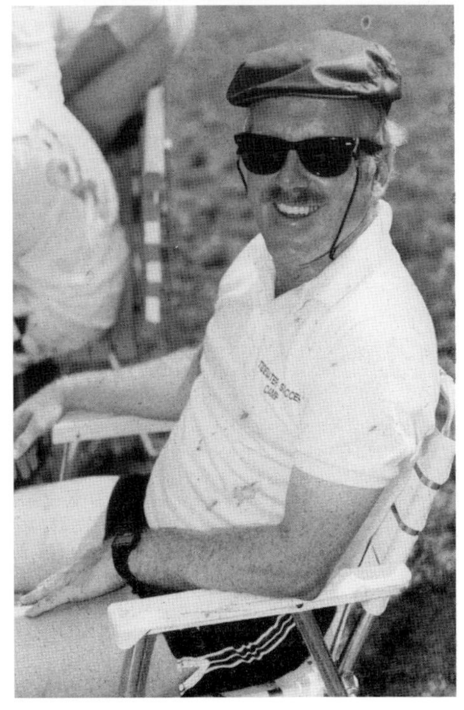

John Daly came to the Tidewater Soccer Camp in 1977 to work summer soccer camps. He became the assistant men's coach in 1979 and eventually worked his way into the women's soccer program as an assistant to John Charles. He became head coach in 1987, and under his leadership, W&M women's soccer has become one of the best college programs in the country.

Campers compete on the "kombikit" on the last day of the Tidewater Soccer Camp. In the last 34 years, over 10,000 youth have attended a session of the camp. In 2007, Chris Norris began the Colonial Kicks Soccer Camp on campus for boys, and John Daly has his John Daly Soccer Camp for young female players.

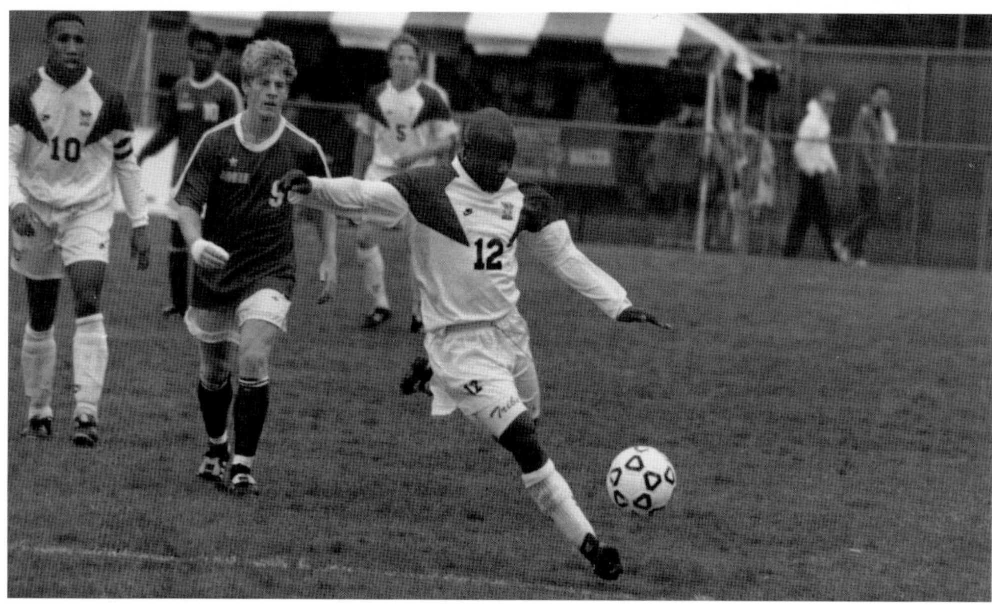

Jon Kamara moves with the ball in a game in the ODU Classic. Kamara came to W&M from Sierra Leone via Indianapolis and was a center midfielder on the outstanding 1992 team. He stayed in Williamsburg after graduation and is now director of the youth academy for the Virginia Legacy Soccer Club, coach at many local camps, and assistant coach for the W&M team.

BUSCH GARDENS - WILLIAM AND MARY

INVITATIONAL SOCCER TOURNAMENT

- BUSCH GARDENS GOLD
- ST. ANDREW'S JUNIOR "B"
- ANNANDALE CAVALIERS
- DIPLOMAT SOCCER CLUB

CARY FIELD, COLLEGE OF WILLIAM AND MARY
WILLIAMSBURG, VA. JUNE 12-13, 1976

OFFICIAL PROGRAM .50

In 1975, Dennis Long, president of Anheuser-Busch, approached W&M soccer to collaborate on a youth tournament so that the Busch club teams from St. Louis could come to Williamsburg in the summer, enjoy some East Coast competition, and have fun at a newly opened theme park, Busch Gardens. This is the cover of the first-ever Busch Gardens–William and Mary Invitational, one of the best youth tournaments in the country for years. Every participant in the tournament received a free ticket to Busch Gardens as part of the event. The Annandale Cavaliers were one of the teams in the first event, and many of the players from their national championship squad helped W&M gain prominence in the late 1970s. The action shots on the cover are from W&M's game against Randolph-Macon, a power in Virginia college soccer in the 1970s. The tournament was a major recruiting event for many East Coast college coaches.

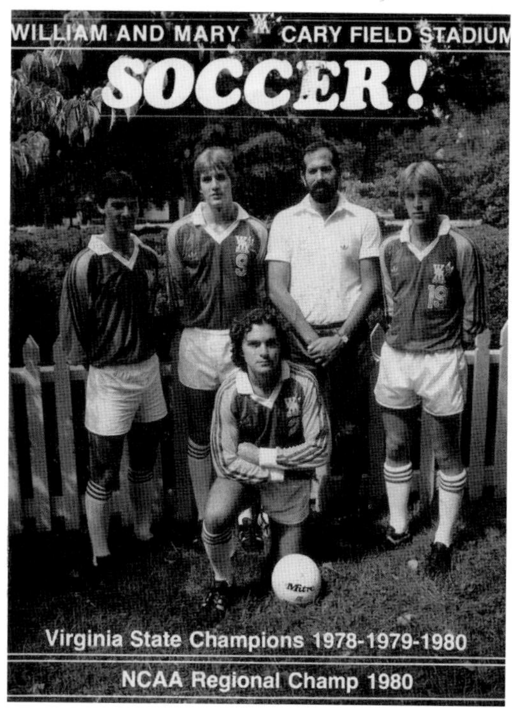

WILLIAM AND MARY
CARY FIELD STADIUM
SOCCER!
Virginia State Champions 1978-1979-1980
NCAA Regional Champ 1980

The 1981 yearbook cover features, from left to right, senior John Chuday, sophomore Thom Sutlive, coach Al Albert, and freshman Keith Exton, with senior Peter Kalaris kneeling in front. Sutlive and Exton were two of the first local players from the Williamsburg Soccer Club to stay at home and build the Tribe to national prominence. Both played in the original Williamsburg Youth Soccer League, for travel soccer teams in the Williamsburg Soccer Club, and for the varsity soccer team at Lafayette High School.

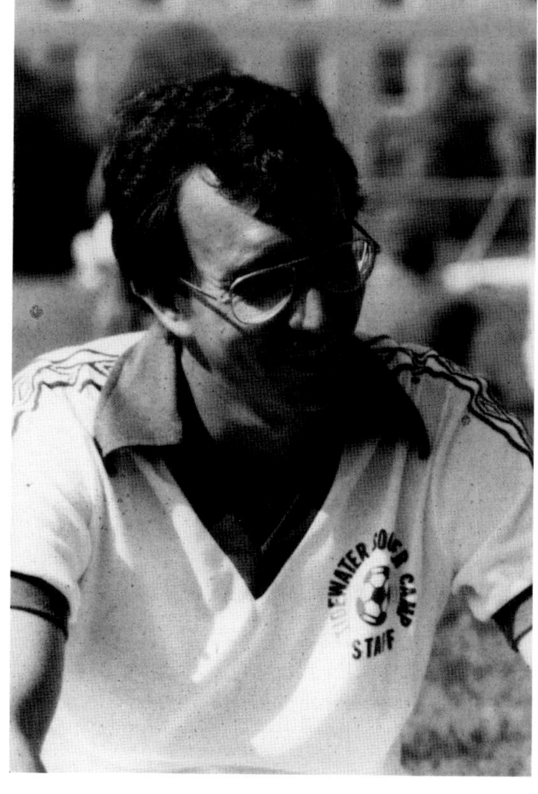

Vins Sutlive III was one of the many coaches at the Tidewater Soccer Camp; he and his brother Thom also played for the Tribe. Vins's father, an anthropology professor at the college, helped start the original youth soccer program in town, the Williamsburg Youth Soccer League. Vins was also one of the early coaches of the Lafayette High School varsity.

WILLIAMSBURG SOCCER CLUB, INC.

P. O. Box 296 Williamsburg, Virginia 23185

To Those Attending Today's Game:

The Williamsburg Soccer Club is pleased to have been asked to join with the College in sponsoring the fourth annual William & Mary Classic Tournament. We also are proud to have contributed to the preparation of this printed program.

During the six year history of our club, of which William & Mary coach Al Albert was a co-founder, we have seen soccer grow strong at the College. Not as a matter of coincidence, our club program has become strong as well. The William & Mary team, student body, its faculty, staff and facilities are directly responsible for our growth and strength.

Many William & Mary students serve as coaches for our teams, all of the founding members of our board of directors were members of the College Faculty and without the College facilities we would not have adequate playing fields.

We hope that our relationship with the College Soccer Program continues and that both of our programs continue to strengthen. We are proud to be part of the William & Mary "Team" and thankful that they are part of our "Club" as well.

We wish them another championship season.

Stuart D. Spirn
President

This letter was in the 1980 W&M Classic game program. The Williamsburg Soccer Club, founded in 1974, has evolved 35 years later into the Virginia Legacy Soccer Club. Stuart Spirn continues as president of the Virginia Legacy, and Al Albert and Chris Norris are board members. Many past players, such as Jon Kamara and Jeff Dominguez, continue to strengthen the coaching staff of the local soccer club. Chris Scrofani also works with young players at the Williamsburg Indoor Sports Center. Among others, Thom Sutlive, Keith Exton, David Schifrin, Andy Crapol, Graham Albert, and Andy Ross all came from the Williamsburg area to play for W&M.

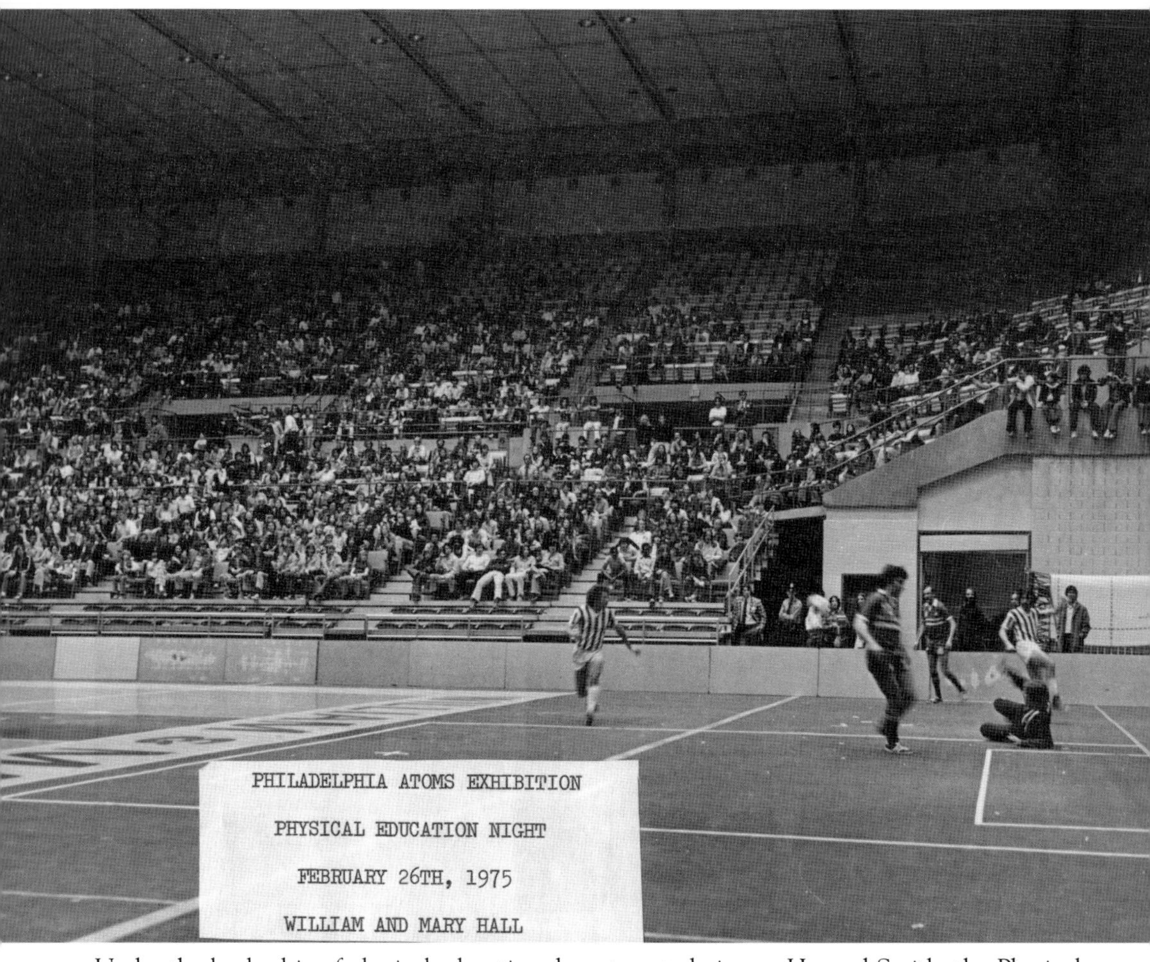

Under the leadership of physical education department chairman Howard Smith, the Physical Education Majors Club chose one event annually to promote. In 1975, to celebrate the growth of soccer on campus, it invited the Philadelphia Atoms professional indoor team to come to Williamsburg to play an all-star team of local players, including some W&M varsity players. Over 2,000 fans showed up to witness the match. Seen in the picture is Atoms goalkeeper Bobby Rigby making a save with team captain Derek Trevis looking on in the background. Shown in front of goal for the local team in the stripes is Ray Laroche, who had been a star at JMU. The match was played on the tartan floor at W&M Hall, with tables forming the walls of the playing area. W&M also promoted an annual college indoor tournament in the hall and an all-night indoor tournament for youth and adults in the community, the Nike Indoor Invitational.

4

Beginnings of National Prominence

In 1980, a Cinderella Tribe soccer squad finally scratched out its first NCAA bid. Their third Virginia State Championship and a competitive schedule earned them an at-large bid to the NCAA tournament. In a 24-team field, they were drawn away to perennial power Howard University, coached by Lincoln Phillips.

Howard had dominated the region for a decade, including a national championship in 1972. Their home field was a dirt field, an intimidating venue in the heart of Washington, D.C. To make things tougher, the Tribe traveled to D.C. only to find the field unplayable due to heavy rains. The game was postponed, and the team had to stay an additional night.

The following day, the game started on the wrong note with an early goal by Howard, signaling a potential rout. However, by halftime the Tribe had answered to tie the score. In an incredible effort, W&M survived the second half plus four 15-minute overtimes to advance to penalty kicks. Substitute Mike Bedell came off the bench after 150 minutes of sitting in the frigid cold to stick away his penalty shot. Goalkeeper Steve Gallop took the final penalty himself to put his team in the final eight against Alabama A&M, the favorite in the entire tournament.

Alabama A&M was virtually an international team with no Americans in the starting lineup. They entered the game undefeated and had amazingly outscored their opponents 86-5 in 18 matches. The epic match at W&M's Cary Field was witnessed by 2,600 paying spectators. In the 90th minute, Alabama A&M's Luke Whitley lobbed a ball over Gallop to send his team to the final four in Miami. It would be 16 years before the Tribe would have another chance to get that close to a final four.

At that point, with only two scholarships, it was a fantastic achievement for W&M to even make it to the 24-team national playoff. As the sport grew, W&M scholarships increased, and as the size of the tournament field also expanded, it would soon become more of a regular occurrence.

Three years later, W&M's second NCAA appearance would occur in very dramatic fashion.

Shown from left to right in this 1980 team shot are the NCAA Regional Champions and NCAA quarterfinalists (first row) coach Al Albert, assistant coach John Daly, Mark Gardiner, Richard Miller, John Chuday, Mike Jones, Joe Crowley, Peter Kalaris, Mike Bedell, and Neil Sherman; (second row) manager Pam Hillery, Paul Crowley, John Bray, Juergen Kloo, Steve Gallop, Thom Sutlive, Dave Lam, Rick Derflinger, Mike Flood, Marty Nickley, Rob Olson, Chris Sartorius, John McManus, and assistant coach Andy Jennings. Missing is Paul Wise. Not only was this team the first to get an NCAA bid, it won the state championship for the third straight time, was the first W&M team to be ranked in the top 20, won more games (14) than any past W&M team, and set the record for most goals scored in a season (58) and most shutouts (9).

Two of the most talented players ever to wear a W&M uniform surround an opponent at Cary Field. Steve Graine is on the right and John McManus on the left. Graine was the sweeper on the 1980 team that went to the NCAA quarterfinals, and McManus still holds the single season scoring record for the Tribe with 27 goals that season.

Steve Gallop was one of four Canadians to come to Williamsburg to help build the program in the 1970s. From the St. Andrews Soccer Club of Toronto and the Toronto Jets men's team, he also played for the under-20 Canadian National Team. Gallop's finest moment was making the decisive penalty kick versus Howard University in the NCAA tournament in 1980.

Soccer America, December 11 1980 25

DIVISION I

Alabama A&M slips past Bill & Mary

By Paul Kennedy

WILLIAMSBURG, VA (Dec. 7)— This was supposed to be a horrible mismatch, Alabama A&M against William & Mary.

With a seasoned team of seven Nigerians, three Jamaicans, and an Ethiopian refugee in the starting lineup, Alabama had outscored its opponents 86-5 in 19 games and done a Zulu dance as a warmup drill that was enough to intimidate the most confident of teams. The experts said that the big, bad Bulldogs would breeze through their schedule and win the NCAA Division I title in their first try. No one would touch A&M, they said, especially not William & Mary which had won only two of its last eight games and survived 60 minutes of overtime to beat Howard with penalty kicks in the first round.

William & Mary coach Al Albert almost admitted as much, likening the matchup to "Rocky III." "We'll try to last and hope for a break," he said before the game.

Well, as the clock ticked down and the Bulldogs missed opportunity after opportunity, it was their 25-year-old coach, Tim Hankinson, who had ants in his pants. "I was starting to say, 'maybe this is our fate, too, the same as Howard's, and it is meant to be an American tournament this year.'" he said.

But as fate would have it, Indian goalie Steve Gallop, who had done as fine a job between the posts as you'd ever want to see, was a split second slow off his line and the Bulldog's Luke Whitley beat him to Gabru Woldeamanuel's cross pass and headed it into the net.

The huge clock overhead read 0:35.

The Bulldogs' 1-0 victory advances them to the NCAA semifinals at Tampa, where they will face San Francisco, a winner over St. Louis U.

Whitley's goal could not have come at a better time, as A&M was notably frustrated by Gallop's heroics, resorting to wild shots from the outside.

"Part of it is a sense of frustration and desperation—let's get a goal somehow," Hankinson explained. "It's also a tactical thing where if you keep pounding to the outside, they're going to leave your strikers and come out at your midfielders. This is going to release the strength at the back. That's how we got a goal. We've taught it as tactics, but whether it is actually frustration I'm not sure.

"They threw us for a loop," added Hankinson. "We were expecting them to play total defense *a la* Duke (which lost 2-0 to A&M in the South regional final). They came out against us. I'm glad they did because it's an exciting game when you play open."

Mark Gardiner, Rob Olson and Paul Wise had good chances for the Indians in the first half. But the A&M defense, led by centerback Douglas Bell, was just too much.

"We don't see too many college games where they just play the game," Hankinson continued. "This game should go down in the books as something all teams should model themselves after."

"Everybody said that Alabama A&M was much better than Howard," Albert commented. "But there is no one around like them. There's only one guy from Howard who could even get onto the team."

Hankinson admitted the Bulldogs will have to be more physical in Tampa and that he will save his best system for the final. . .if they can get past USF.

William & Mary coach Al Albert (right) was elated after his team's upset of Howard, but not too happy after the Indians dropped an NCAA quarter-final match to Alabama A&M (Photo by John Albino)

NCAA DIVISION I PLAYOFFS AT A GLANCE
Quarter-final Round:
USF 3, St. Louis 2
Alabama A&M 1 William & Mary 0
Hartwick 1, Connecticut 0 (2 OT)
Indiana 3, Penn State 1

Semi-final Round:
Dec. 13 at Tampa, Florida
Hartwick vs. Indiana
USF vs. Alabama A&M
Finals: Dec. 14 @ Tampa

This *Soccer America* article details the amazing game between the Tribe and Alabama A&M in the NCAA quarterfinal played at Cary Field. It is unlikely that NCAA Division I soccer will see an international team of the stature of A&M any time soon under the present recruiting restrictions. The quarterfinal match with the Bulldogs at home generated more attention for the W&M soccer program than at any previous point. The *Washington Post* began its postgame article with the line, "Playing with all the heart and courage of a team that has faced adversity all year, William and Mary battled a more talented and experienced Alabama A&M team for 89:25 minutes before succumbing 1-0." The NCAA tournament ran later than it does now, and this game is the only one ever played by a Tribe team in December. Ironically, the weather was unseasonably warm and the daytime game temperature was over 80 degrees, even though it had been quite cold for the Howard game one week earlier. (Courtesy of Lynn Berling.)

Mark Gardiner steadied the Tribe midfield from 1977 to 1981, missing his sophomore year due to injury. Gardiner also played for the silver-medal-winning U.S. Maccabiah team in the summer of 1981. Although hampered by knee issues most of his career, his tremendous work rate was a huge factor for Tribe success during this period.

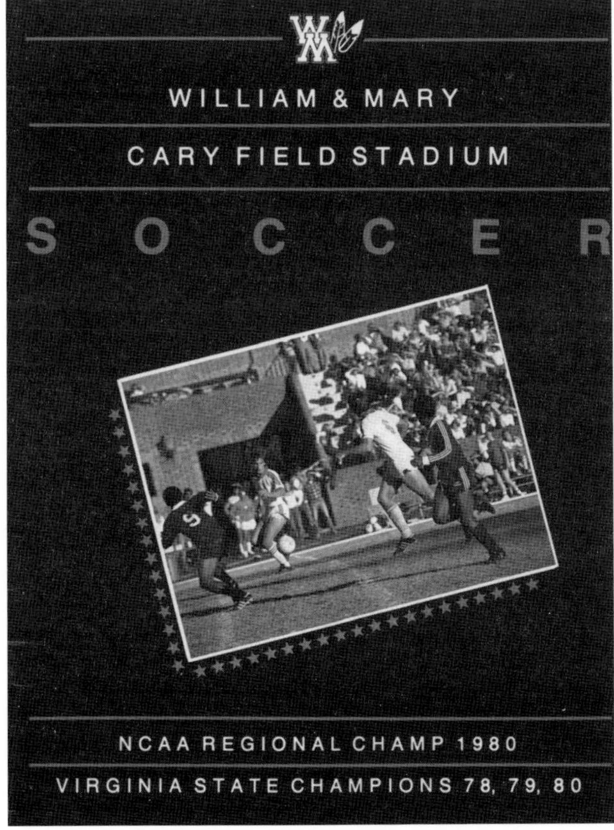

WILLIAM & MARY
CARY FIELD STADIUM
SOCCER
NCAA REGIONAL CHAMP 1980
VIRGINIA STATE CHAMPIONS 78, 79, 80

The 1982 yearbook cover features midfielder Mike Flood passing to fullback Mike Zwicklbauer during a game at Cary Field. Flood, the only freshman starter on the 1980 team, would prove to be a major force and leader for the team his next three years. He now runs one of the largest food banks in the United States in the Los Angeles area. Zwicklbauer is a plastic surgeon locally and works with the Tribe athletic department.

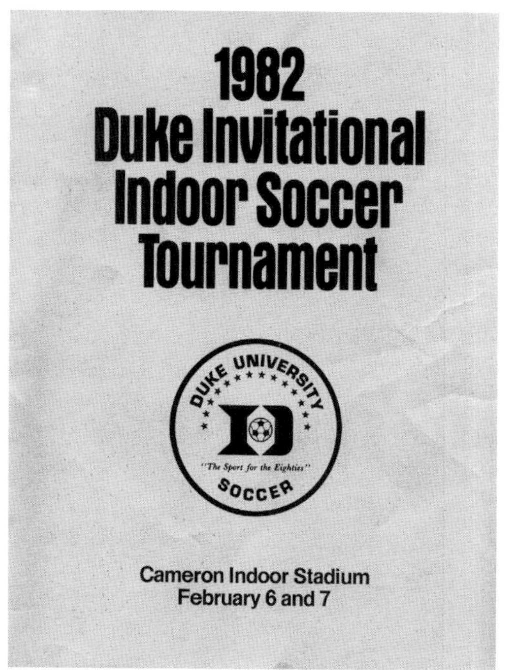

1982
Duke Invitational
Indoor Soccer
Tournament
DUKE UNIVERSITY
"The Sport for the Eighties"
SOCCER
Cameron Indoor Stadium
February 6 and 7

Probably the only time a men's soccer team will ever play in Duke University's Cameron Indoor Stadium was the Duke Indoor Invitational in 1982. Indoor soccer was very popular among the state colleges until the NCAA changed the rules regarding the number of spring semester competitions. Some of the other schools in the tourney were UVA, UNC, NC State, and Wake Forest.

Juergen Kloo took over the goalkeeping reins from Steve Gallop after the 1980 season and was team MVP his senior year in 1982. He led the 1981 and 1982 teams to a combined 26-9-7 record, including a 0-0 tie with defending national champion UConn at Cary Field to open the 1982 season.

Marty Nickley, the captain of the outstanding 1980 team, was an imposing stopper from Northern Virginia who walked on to the team in 1977. On Cary's narrow field, he was a tremendous presence in the middle of the defense, a very tough tackler, and strong in the air. After graduation, Marty has been the longtime soccer coach at T. C. Williams High School in the D.C. area, where he teaches mathematics.

Andy (Smolin) Sutton challenges a UConn player in the 1982 season opener at Cary Field against the national champions from the previous season. The game ended in a 0-0 draw. In the background is Mark Goldberg, an English player who played two years for the Tribe in 1982 and 1983.

Todd Middlebrook (1981–1984) was a key player for the Tribe in the center of the midfield and would ultimately captain the team. He was the winner of the Coaches' Award in 1983 and was voted MVP by his teammates in 1984. Todd was also All–ECAC South his senior year.

The 1982 team put together a solid 11-5-4 record but lost to UVA 1-0 in the VIL playoffs. A highlight of the season was a trip to Tampa for the University of South Florida Invitational. The Tribe tied 1-1 a strong USF squad, which was led by future pro Roy Wegerle.

5

BACK TO THE SHOW

The 1983 season had been a roller-coaster year. The Tribe had suffered its worst defeat in years, an 8-2 drubbing at Duke, followed by an incredible 1-0 upset of the UConn in Storrs, Connecticut. The goal in Storrs was scored by Jon Stewart, the biggest goal of his W&M career.

On the last day of the season, W&M's Mike Flood found himself in a one-on-one breakaway at the George Mason goal with seconds to go. Flood calmly slotted the goal away to give W&M its first ECAC South championship and, more importantly, its second-ever NCAA bid. Its opponent this time would be powerful UVA, led by a young, up-and-coming coach, Bruce Arena.

The game was set for Scott Stadium, the cavernous football stadium in Charlottesville. The field, a hard, worn Astroturf surface, was not the best situation for the Tribe. It was a great opportunity, however, for the program to again prove itself at the highest level of college soccer.

The game started uneventfully, and at halftime, the score stood at 0-0. Early in the second half, a tremendous downpour slowed play but did not halt the game. Two second-half goals sank the Tribe, the first of which was scored off of a long-flip throw by the Cavaliers' Voga Wallace. The throw from in front of the Tribe bench skimmed off a defender's head directly into the net. W&M's Scott Bell scored a late goal to make the final score 2-1.

The final NCAA appearance of the decade came at the end of the 1987 season. William and Mary again clinched the CAA title with a 3-0 win at JMU on the last day of October. It carried some injuries into the postseason, however, and lost a disappointing 1-0 game at Loyola in Baltimore in the first round of the NCAA.

At that point, virtually every Tribe player since 1980 had been on a team that made it to NCAA postseason play. That was something to be proud of, but beginning in 1992, postseason competition would become a much more common occurrence.

1983 WILLIAM AND MARY SOCCER

NCAA REGIONAL FINALIST
ECAC SOUTH CHAMPIONS

The 1983 team won the ECAC South title and returned to the NCAA in dramatic fashion. Shown above, from left to right, are (first row) John Rasnic, Tom Erdmann, Bob Mageras, Scott Repke, Andy Watson, Andy (Smolin) Sutton, Scott Bell, Darcy Curran, and Richard Miller; (second row) Larry Crisman, Dan Sheehan, Bob Ageloff, Coach Albert, Coach Daly, Nancy Love Williams, Lance Holland, and Mike Zwicklbauer; (third row) Keith Exton, Glenn Livingstone, Todd Middlebrook, Dave Snyder, Thom Sutlive, Hart Baur, Mike Flood, Rich Miranda, and Mike Kalaris. Missing from the photograph are Charles Smith, Mark Goldberg, and Jon (Leibowitz) Stewart. Below the team celebrates a goal at Cary Field.

Date: 11/12/83 **THE SOCCER SCOREBOOK** by L.A.W., Ltd. Referees

Match No. ECAC South

HOME W&M 4 VISITOR George Mason 3

shot	asst	goal	STARTERS	No	POSITION	No	STARTERS	shot	asst	goal
			Smith	GK	keeper	GK	Stames			
			Watson	4	defense	23	Burrell			
II			Livingstone	17		22	McDermott			
			Curran	14		19	Thompson	I		I
			Repke	15	midfield	14	Kerr (yellow)	IIII	I	II
IIIIIII	I		Flood	6		4	Reynolds	I		I
			Kalaris	8		7	Lemair	II		
I		I	Middlebrook	20	forwards	8	Duffy			
II			Smolin	13		10	West			
I			Leibowitz	12		18	McIntyre			
			Bell	19		6	Jung			
I			Goldberg	15	Substitutes	3	Skeffington	I		
		II	Crisman	2		5	Minshew			
III			Exton	10		11	Hay			
			Miller	7		9		I		

TOTALS	W&M		George Mason	
shots		22		11
saves		6		13
corner kicks		8		3

team	goal	assist	time
W&M	Middlebrook	—	13:45
GMU	Reynolds	Kerr	41:27
GMU	Kerr	-	62:57
GMU	Thompson	Kerr	63:45
W&M	Crisman	-	82:40
WM	Crisman	Leibowitz	82:55
W&M	Flood		109:36

All Rights Reserved

The ECAC South final was one of the greatest games in Tribe soccer history. Earlier in the regular season, George Mason had come to Williamsburg and lost 2-1 on two goals in the last 10 minutes. Mason had to be thinking about this as it came back to Cary in November. The Patriots led 3-1 late in the game, as goals by their three most dangerous players—Fred Thompson, Mike Reynolds, and Colin Kerr—trumped the opening goal by W&M's Todd Middlebrook. Kerr even hit the post late in the game, which could have given his team a 4-1 advantage. Amazingly, lightning struck again. Two goals within 15 seconds by Larry Crisman, a substitute forward who had scored the game winner in the earlier match, brought the match to overtime. Then, with only 24 seconds to go, Mike Flood scored the goal (shown on the back cover) to give the Tribe a league championship and an NCAA bid.

W&M had traveled to almost every game in vans in the 1983 season. When it won the ECAC South, it meant a trip back to the NCAA tourney in a chartered bus. The travel dress code was upgraded to coat and tie; this picture was taken at Scott Stadium the day before the game. Today Howard Smith (third row, far left), who was driving this bus for the Newton Bus Company, owns the Oleta Bus Company in Williamsburg, which drives Tribe men's soccer to all away games. Below, Howard poses in front of one of his fleet of coaches.

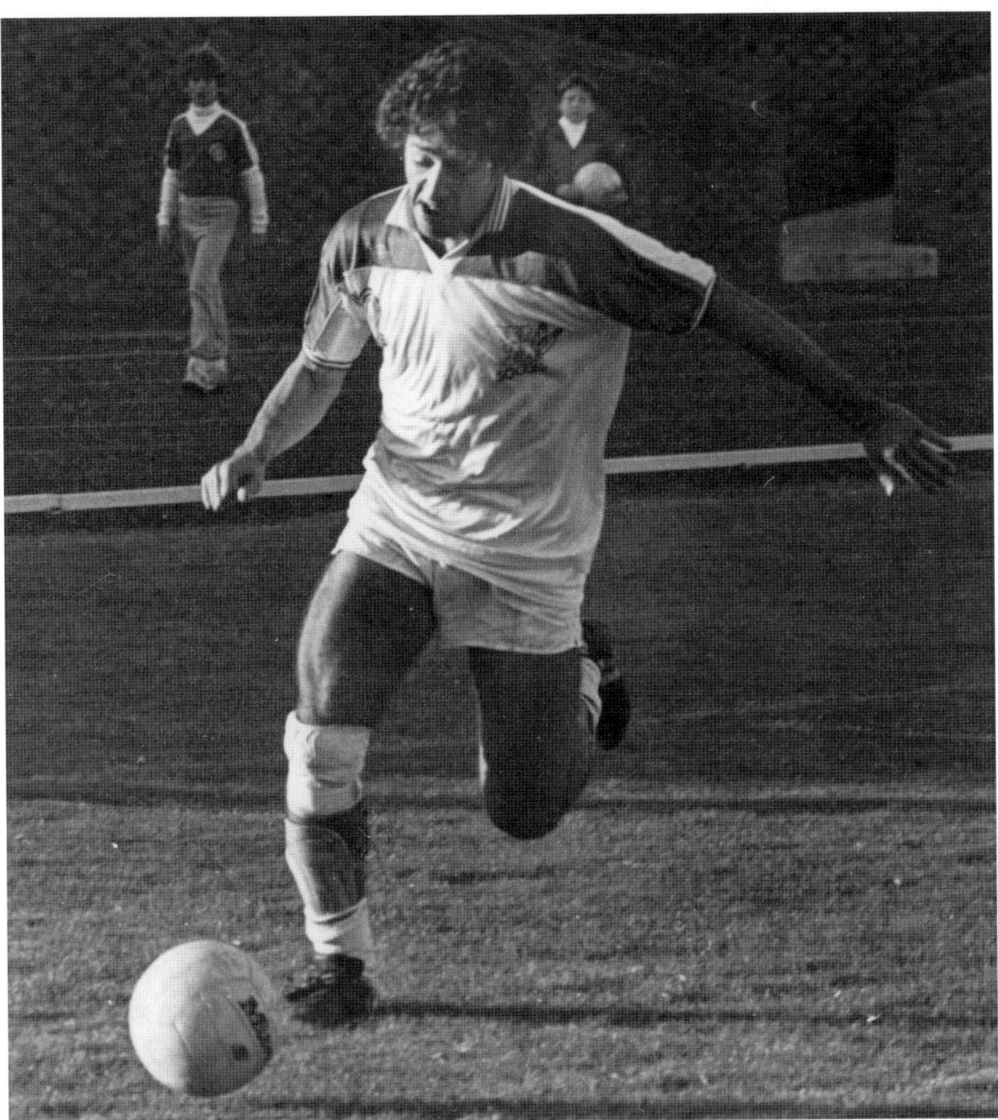

Jon Stewart dribbles to goal in a game at Cary Field. The young ball boy in the background is David Schifrin, who went on to play sweeper for the Tribe from 1992 to 1995. Jon, known as "Leibo" to his teammates, walked on to the program in 1980 and played junior varsity club soccer that year. He joined the varsity as a sophomore and quickly became a starter on the wing. He finished his career with 12 assists, which at that time put him on the top-10 career-assist list for the program. In the summer of 1983, before his senior season, he played for the U.S. squad, which won the silver medal in the first Pan-American Maccabi Games in Sao Paulo, Brazil. Perhaps his biggest moment was in 1983, when he scored the lone goal in a 1-0 upset of powerful UConn in Storrs, Connecticut. After that season, Stewart considered using his fourth season of eligibility or playing professional indoor soccer but gave in to some nagging neck and knee injuries. His decision to give up soccer and concentrate on comedy seems to have been a great career move.

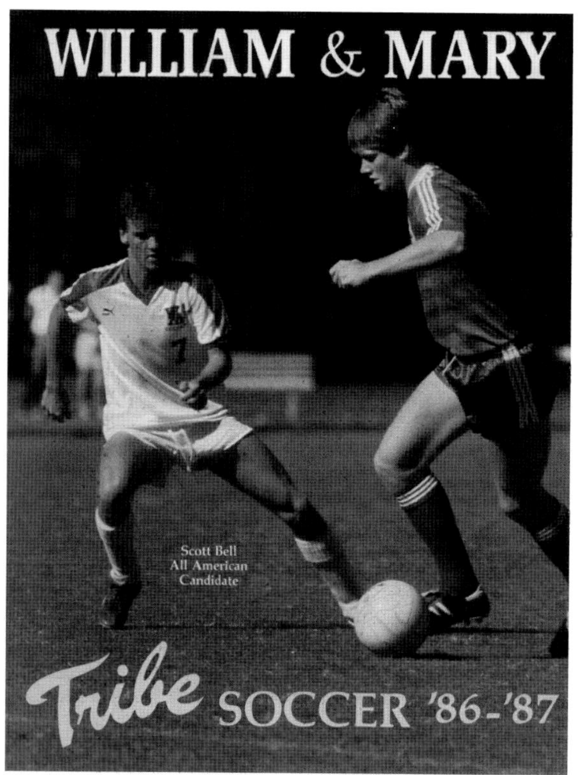

WILLIAM & MARY
Scott Bell
All American
Candidate
Tribe SOCCER '86-'87

Scott Bell challenges Doug Bradley, son of legendary George Mason soccer coach Gordon Bradley, for the ball. Bell finished his career with 46 goals, at that time the most in school history, despite missing 10 games his senior year. Scott was the last of six Canadian players to help the Tribe to national prominence during this period. He later played professional indoor soccer for Dallas.

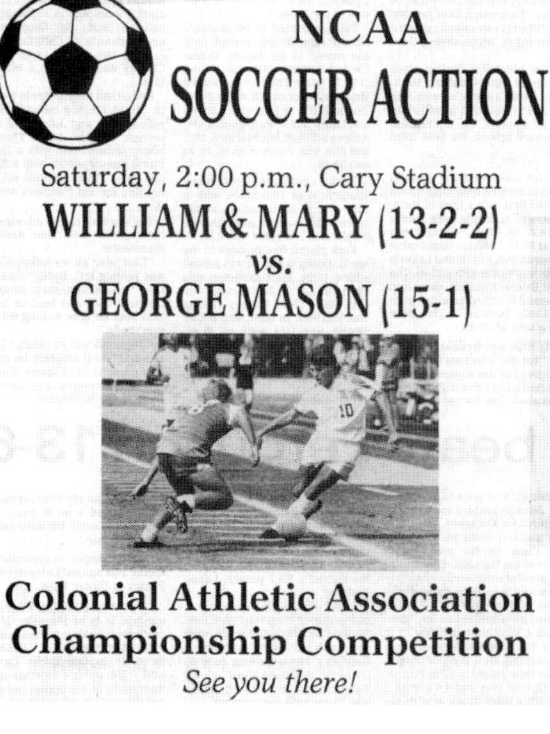

NCAA
SOCCER ACTION
Saturday, 2:00 p.m., Cary Stadium
WILLIAM & MARY (13-2-2)
vs.
GEORGE MASON (15-1)
Colonial Athletic Association
Championship Competition
See you there!

An advertisement from the *Virginia Gazette* promotes the regular season game between W&M and George Mason in 1985. Unfortunately the Tribe lost to the Patriots 4-2, dashing its hopes for an NCAA bid. Between 1984 and 1986, the Tribe posted solid winning seasons, but it failed to clinch another NCAA bid until 1987.

Jon Tuttle takes on George Mason's Mike Reynolds. Both Tuttle and Reynolds were named to the CAA's silver anniversary all-star team. Tuttle and Scott Bell paired to form a potent attack for the Tribe in the late 1980s. As a left-sided player, Tuttle created many goal-scoring situations for the Tribe. Jon played briefly for the Boston Bolts of the American Soccer League while a law student at Harvard.

Tim Larkin played for the Tribe from 1984 to 1987 and was captain his senior year. He had been named best rookie as a freshman and received the Coaches' Award as a junior. He was named CAA Player of the Week on October 5, 1987. Following his W&M career, he played briefly with Fort Wayne of the American Professional Soccer League (indoor) and presently is a professional sports event manager.

'87 - '88 Tribe

nt Row (l. to r.): Summer Hambrick, Don Dichiara, Tim Larkin, Doug Annakin, Ian Peter, Bo Eskay, Steve Kokulis, Paul Bjarn Murcia and Michael Cummings. Second Row (l. to r.): Marty Taylor, Jon Tuttle, Ali Ghassemi, Steve Szczypinski, Conor F on Katner, Joel Lewin, Mike Repke and Head Coach Al Albert. Third Row (l. to r.): Lou McGranaghan (trainer), Rich Spencer, han, Jonas Cedergren, Ron Raab, Bruce Ensley, Larry Valentine and Assistant Coach Mike Flood.

After three years of falling short, the 1987 Tribe clinched the CAA title and an automatic NCAA bid with two weeks to go in the season. It was only the second year that the young league had an automatic bid, one of only five conferences at that time to qualify (now there are over 20). Unfortunately the Tribe went into the first-round match with Loyola carrying some key injuries and lost to the Greyhounds in Baltimore 1-0. Its final record was 14-5-2. Welshman Ian Peter had an outstanding season in goal his senior year. Ron Raab led all scorers with nine goals, trailed by Ricky Dahan with eight and Jon Tuttle with seven. W&M lost tough regular-season games to ODU and George Mason but swept Central Florida and South Florida on its fall break trip. Ricky Dahan was named CAA Player of the Year.

6

Consistent Postseason Play

From 1988 to 1991, Tribe soccer posted consistent winning seasons but failed to break through to NCAA postseason play. In 1989, the team had moved into its new home at Busch Field, an Astroturf shared-use facility behind W&M Hall. Cary Field had been the site of many great games but having a field for all weather conditions was a big step for the Tribe, and being able to play on campus under the lights meant a huge spike in attendance.

In the 1992 season, led by seniors Scott Budnick and Khary Stockton, W&M had an 18-game unbeaten streak and at one point was ranked third in the National Soccer Coaches Association of America (NSCAA) national poll, to this date its highest ranking ever. Not only did the Tribe get into the NCAA field in 1992, it was given its first home game since the 1980 playoff with Alabama A&M. The game versus WVU at Busch Field was won by W&M 2-0. It would be 16 years before another NCAA men's soccer game would come to Williamsburg because of the Astroturf surface.

From 1992 to 2003, the Tribe only missed NCAA play twice. In 1994, the 18-3-1 CAA runners-up were stunned by their omission from the selections by the NCAA committee. They had been ranked nationally all season long, but this was prior to the RPI (ratings percentage index), and no one, including the coaches, had any idea that they were not in a good position to make the tournament. It was a painful lesson for players and coaches.

In 2004, W&M soccer moved to Albert-Daly Field, ironically steps from the original site of the first field and the Lions Jamboree. The new facility, made possible by a generous gift from Jim and Bobbie Ukrop of Richmond, consisted of a state-of-the-art Bermuda grass field and lighting.

From 2004 to 2007, there was a bit of a drought in qualifying for NCAA post-season, but finally in 2008, W&M was selected at-large and made it to the second round of the playoffs, losing an overtime game to powerful Wake Forest University in Winston-Salem, North Carolina. It also hosted its first NCAA game in 16 years, a 3-1 win over Big South champions Winthrop University.

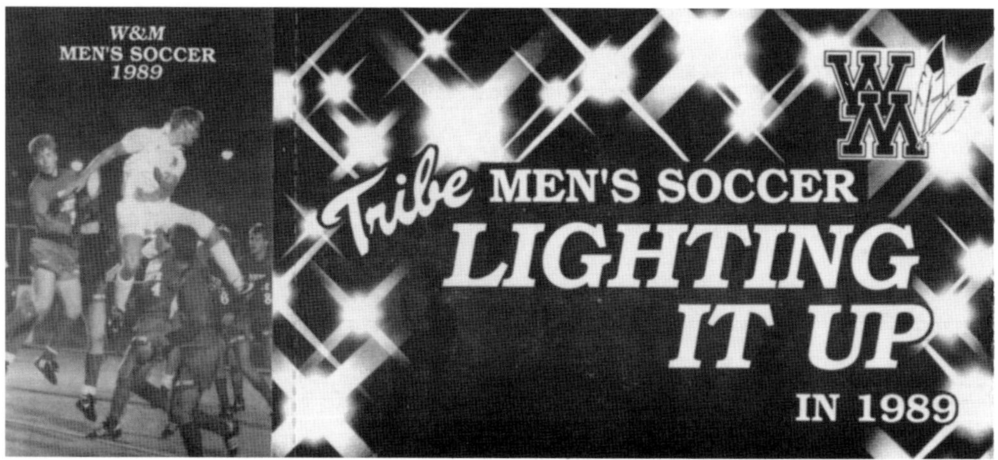

In 1989, W&M soccer moved into Busch Field, a new Astroturf facility behind W&M Hall. Playing on campus and under the lights, crowds improved dramatically. The opener at Busch Field was a 2-1 win over Davidson in front of a packed house. On the cover of this season ticket brochure, Paul Bjarnason heads the ball away during a game against Ohio State in the Met Life Classic at ODU's Foreman Field.

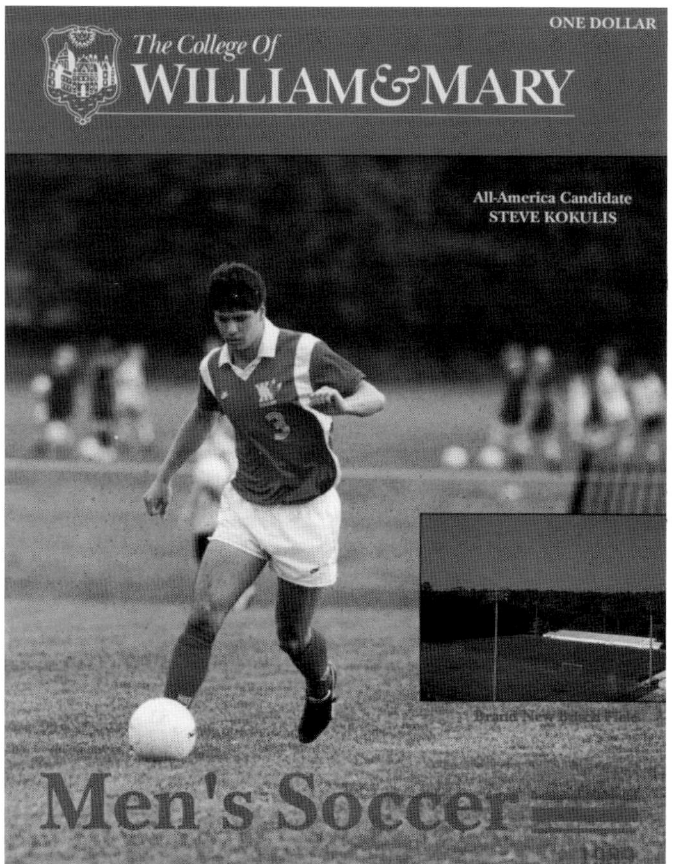

Steve Kokulis, pictured on the cover of the 1989 media guide, was one of the top defenders in the history of the program. Known for his great timing and ferocious tackling, Steve was a mainstay as sweeper for his four years in Williamsburg. He was team MVP in 1989 and was selected to play in the East-West Senior Bowl. He was also named to the All–South Atlantic regional team in 1988 and 1989. Also shown on the cover in the inset is an overhead picture of brand-new Busch Field.

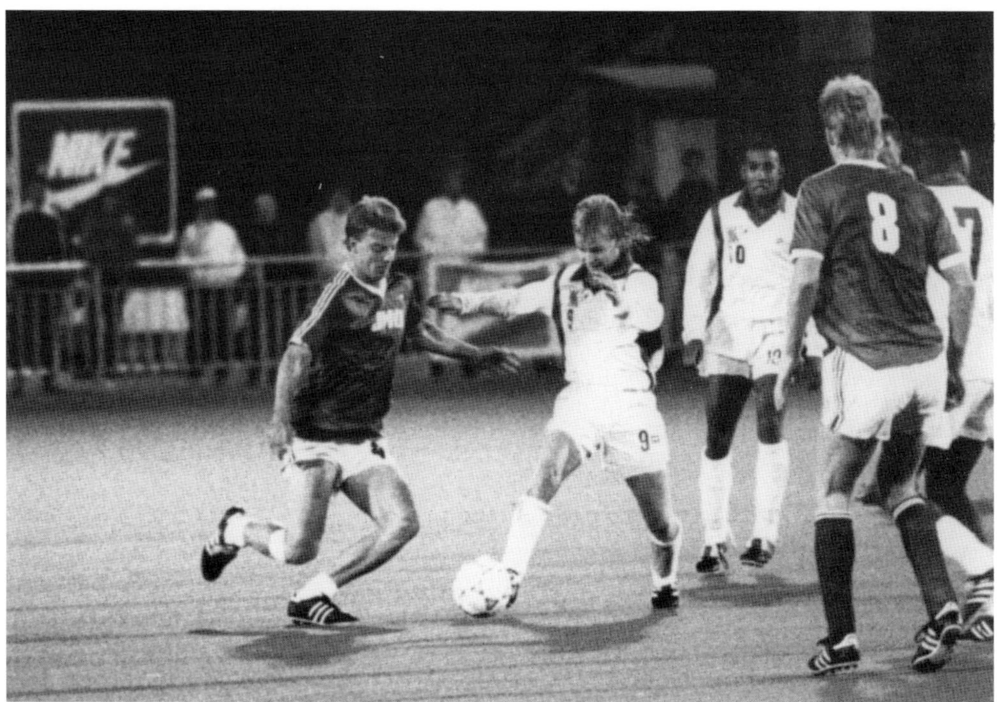

Midfielder Greg Butler challenges for a ball from a JMU player at a game at Busch Field in 1990 as Khary Stockton watches in the background. Butler was a transfer from Boston University who played two years for the Tribe from 1990 to 1991. The Tribe finished 11-6-3 in 1990 but lost to Navy 3-2 in the CAA tournament at Richmond to end its season.

Kieran McCarthy receives the team championship trophy from Charles Plisko of Pizza Hut in the Pizza Hut Classic in 1990. McCarthy was All-CAA in 1990 and 1991 and anchored the Tribe backline during that period. He also received the team's Coaches' Award (now called the Crapol Award) for his attitude and team spirit in 1989.

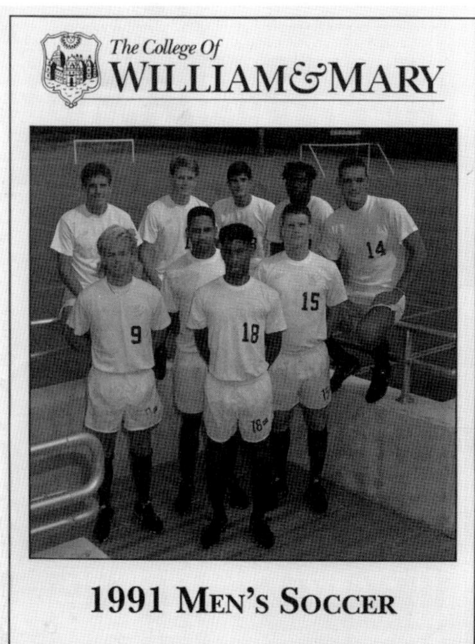

The College Of
WILLIAM&MARY
1991 MEN'S SOCCER

The cover of the 1991 yearbook shows the large senior class at Busch Field: from left to right are (first row) Gregg Butler and Scott Williams; (second row) David Starks and John Siner; (third row) Jimmy Hauschild, Kieran McCarthy, Dave Viscovich, Mo Smith, and Mike Cummings. Unfortunately when the cover picture was shot, the game uniforms had not arrived. The white practice shirts and white game shorts make this look more like an underwear ad than a soccer team.

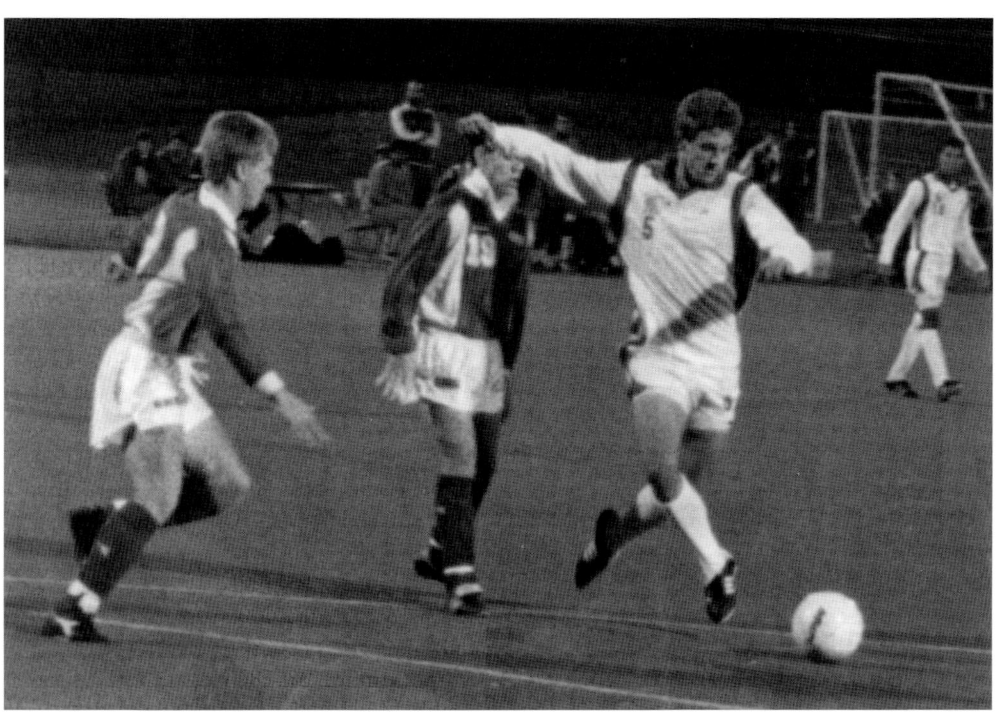

Jimmy Hauschild, one of the most technical players ever to play in the backline for W&M, is shown in a game at Busch Field in 1991. Hauschild was named All–South Atlantic in 1990 and 1991 and was a four-year All-CAA selection. The 1991 team was 11-7-3 but lost to JMU in the CAA tournament in Norfolk.

Mike Cummings was the MVP of the 1991 team. A highly touted recruit, he struggled early in his career for playing time and also battled an illness that forced him to drop out of school for a semester. Returning at 100 percent, he worked himself into a starting position as an outside midfielder and finished his career with five goals and three assists his senior season.

Dave Viscovich was a second-team All-CAA midfielder in 1990 and 1991. "Chico" was a four year starter from 1988 to 1991. He scored six goals as a midfielder in each of his last two seasons for the Tribe.

Led by seniors Scott Budnick and Khary Stockton, the 1992 team achieved the highest national ranking in program history, No. 3 in the NSCAA poll. After a 1-3 start, they were 14-0-4 in their next 18 games. Highlighting that 18-game unbeaten run were ties with national powers UVA and UCLA. They finished with a 15-5-4 record and made it to the second round of the NCAA tournament. Shown here, from left to right, are (first row) Brian Reshefsky, David Schifrin, Andrew Petty, Chris Scrofani, Tim Prisco, Scott Budnick, Chris Drescher, Paul Grafer, Billy Owens, Jason Zawacki, Greg Richards, and Mulumba Tshishimbi; (second row) Chris Norris, Christian Powers, Andy Chapin, Khary Stockton, Guy Cartwright, coach Mike Cummings, coach Al Albert, coach Steve Shaw, Greg Turk, Eric Dumbleton, Joe Soos, Joe McGovern, John Mohseni, and Jon Kamara. Missing is coach Seth Roland.

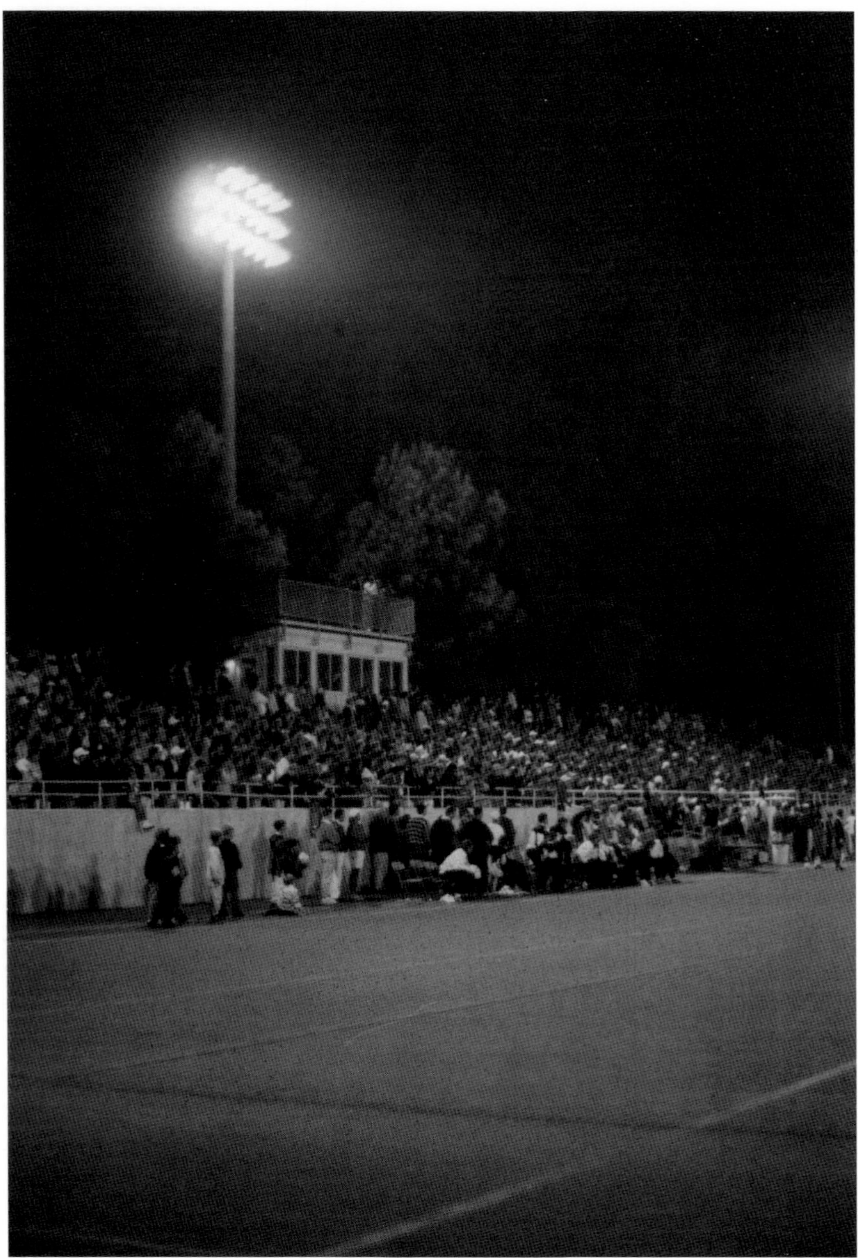

In 1992, W&M welcomed a strong UVA team to Busch Field. The Cavalier squad included such future greats as Claudio Reyna, and it went on to win its second straight national title that year. UVA was hoping to set its program's consecutive wins record by beating the Tribe but was only able to come away with a 0-0 tie. After the game, UVA coach Bruce Arena publicly criticized W&M for not more aggressively seeking a win, but the Tribe went on to be ranked higher than Virginia in a subsequent national poll and make the NCAA tournament for the first time in five years. The 1992 squad was a terrifically overachieving team that set the standard for future performance.

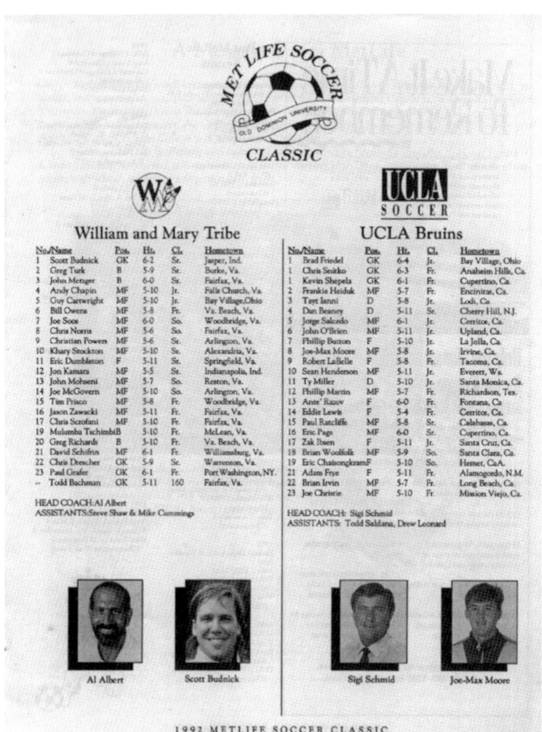

MET LIFE SOCCER
OLD DOMINION UNIVERSITY
CLASSIC

UCLA SOCCER

William and Mary Tribe

No.	Name	Pos.	Ht.	Cl.	Hometown
1	Scott Budnick	GK	6-2	Sr.	Jasper, Ind.
2	Greg Turk	B	5-9	Sr.	Burke, Va.
3	John Metzger	B	6-0	Sr.	Fairfax, Va.
4	Andy Chapin	MF	5-10	Jr.	Falls Church, Va.
5	Guy Cartwright	MF	5-10	Jr.	Bay Village,Ohio
6	Bill Owens	MF	5-8	Fr.	Va. Beach, Va.
7	Joe Soos	MF	6-0	So.	Woodbridge, Va.
8	Chris Norris	MF	5-6	So.	Fairfax, Va.
9	Christian Powers	MF	5-6	Sr.	Arlington, Va.
10	Khary Stockton	MF	5-10	Sr.	Alexandria, Va.
11	Eric Dumbleton	F	5-11	Sr.	Springfield, Va.
12	Jon Kamara	MF	5-5	Sr.	Indianapolis, Ind.
13	John Mohseni	MF	5-7	So.	Reston, Va.
14	Joe McGovern	MF	5-10	So.	Arlington, Va.
15	Tim Prisco	MF	5-8	Fr.	Woodbridge, Va.
16	Jason Zawacki	MF	5-11	Fr.	Fairfax, Va.
17	Chris Scrofani	MF	5-10	Fr.	Fairfax, Va.
19	Mulumba Tschimbi	B	5-10	Fr.	McLean, Va.
20	Greg Richards	B	5-10	Fr.	Va. Beach, Va.
21	David Schifrin	MF	6-1	Fr.	Williamsburg, Va.
22	Chris Drescher	GK	5-9	Sr.	Warrenton, Va.
23	Paul Grafer	GK	6-1	Fr.	Port Washington, NY.
--	Todd Bachman	GK	5-11	160	Fairfax, Va.

HEAD COACH: Al Albert
ASSISTANTS: Steve Shaw & Mike Cummings

UCLA Bruins

No.	Name	Pos.	Ht.	Cl.	Hometown
1	Brad Friedel	GK	6-4	Jr.	Bay Village, Ohio
1	Chris Snitko	GK	6-3	Fr.	Anaheim Hills, Ca.
1	Kevin Shepela	GK	6-1	Fr.	Cupertino, Ca.
2	Frankie Heiduk	MF	5-7	Fr.	Encinitas, Ca.
3	Tayt Ianni	D	5-8	Jr.	Lodi, Ca
4	Dan Beaney	D	5-11	Sr.	Cherry Hill, N.J.
5	Jorge Salcedo	MF	6-1	Jr.	Cerritos, Ca.
6	John O'Brien	MF	5-11	Jr.	Upland, Ca.
7	Phillip Button	F	5-10	Jr.	La Jolla, Ca.
8	Joe-Max Moore	MF	5-8	Jr.	Irvine, Ca.
9	Robert LaBelle	F	5-8	Fr.	Tacoma, Ca.
10	Sean Henderson	MF	5-11	Jr.	Everett, Wa.
11	Ty Miller	D	5-10	Jr.	Santa Monica, Ca.
12	Phillip Martin	MF	5-7	Fr.	Richardson, Tex.
13	Ante' Razov	F	6-0	Fr.	Fontana, Ca
14	Eddie Lewis	F	5-4	Fr.	Cerritos, Ca.
15	Paul Ratcliffe	MF	5-8	Sr.	Calabasas, Ca.
16	Eric Page	MF	6-0	Sr.	Cupertino, Ca.
17	Zak Ibsen	F	5-11	Jr.	Santa Cruz, Ca.
18	Brian Woolfolk	MF	5-9	So.	Santa Clara, Ca.
19	Eric Chaisongkram	F	5-10	So.	Hemet, CaA.
21	Adam Frye	F	5-11	Fr.	Alamogordo, N.M.
22	Brian Irvin	MF	5-7	Fr.	Long Beach, Ca.
23	Joe Christie	MF	5-10	Fr.	Mission Viejo, Ca.

HEAD COACH: Sigi Schmid
ASSISTANTS: Todd Saldana, Drew Leonard

Al Albert
Scott Budnick
Sigi Schmid
Joe-Max Moore

1992 METLIFE SOCCER CLASSIC

The page is from the 1992 ODU Met Life Classic matchup between W&M and powerful UCLA. In the only meeting between the two teams, the Tribe held on for a 0-0 tie. UCLA's roster boasts future national team and professional stars Brad Friedel, Frankie Heyduk, Tayt Ianni, Jorge Salcedo, Joe-Max Moore, Sean Henderson, Ante Razov, Eddie Lewis, and Zak Ibsen.

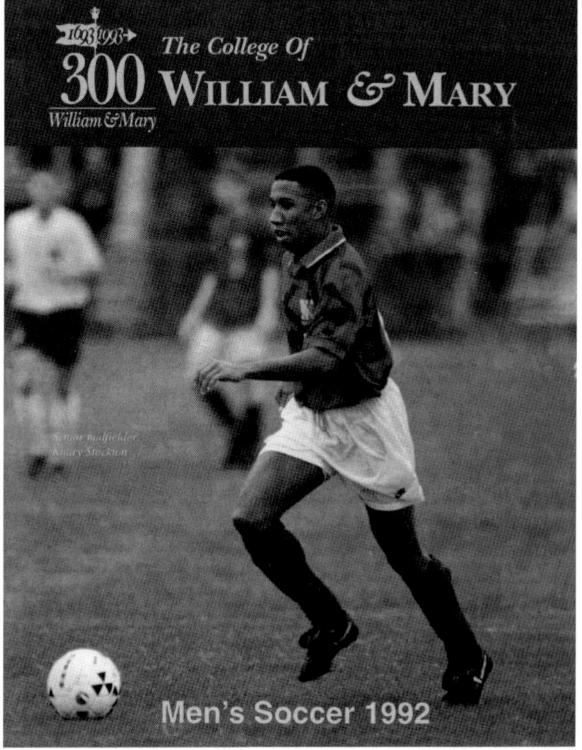

1693 1993
300
William & Mary
The College Of
William & Mary
Men's Soccer 1992

The cover of the 1992 media guide features Khary Stockton, who played a key role in the team's return to the NCAA tournament that year. Khary went on to play professional soccer for a number of teams, most notably the Richmond Kickers, who won the United Soccer Leagues (USL) Division 2 title in 2006. He presently is the head coach at the University of the District of Columbia (UDC).

The cover of the 1992 program for the NCAA second-round match between W&M and Atlantic Coast Conference (ACC) power NC State highlights NC State star Scott Schweitzer. The week prior, the Tribe had defeated WVU 2-0 at Busch Field in the first NCAA playoff game at home since 1980. Eric Dumbleton (below) had scored both goals versus WVU but was sent off late in the NC State game. The Tribe, playing a man down, had a chance to tie late in the game, but the Wolfpack goalkeeper saved a penalty kick, and NC State held on to advance.

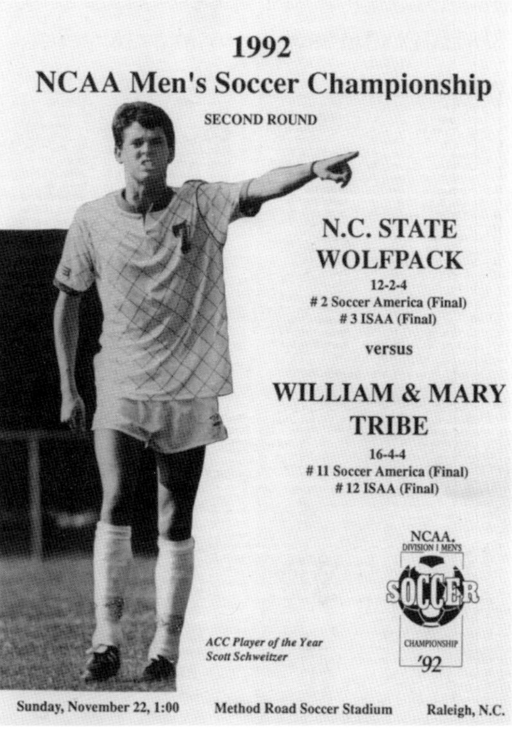

1992
NCAA Men's Soccer Championship
SECOND ROUND

N.C. STATE WOLFPACK
12-2-4
2 Soccer America (Final)
3 ISAA (Final)

versus

WILLIAM & MARY TRIBE
16-4-4
11 Soccer America (Final)
12 ISAA (Final)

NCAA. DIVISION I MEN'S SOCCER CHAMPIONSHIP '92

ACC Player of the Year
Scott Schweitzer

Sunday, November 22, 1:00 Method Road Soccer Stadium Raleigh, N.C.

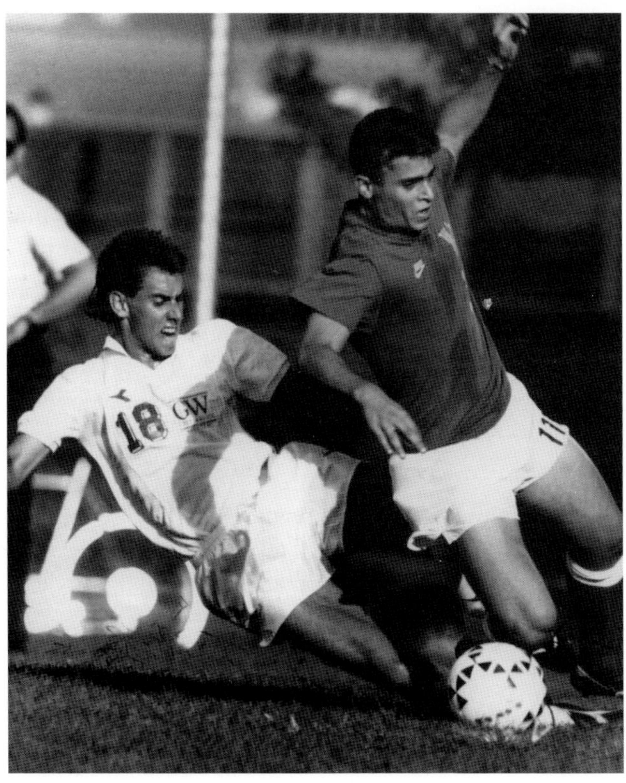

Meet the Tribe

1993 Men's Soccer Team: (left to right) Front Row – Greg Richards, Chris Scrofani, David Schifrin, Guy Cartwright, John Metzger, Andy Chapin, Chris Norris, Billy Owens; Second Row – Jason Zawacki, Tim Prisco, Brian Reshefsky, Steve Jolley, Joe Soos, Joe McGovern, Rob Bryden, Greg Westfall; Third Row – Waughn Hughes, Michael Botta, John Mohseni, Nelson Warley, Desmond McCarthy, Mulumba Tshishimbi, Josh Quinter, Andrew Petty; Back Row – Scott Powers, Asst. Coach Chris Drescher, Head Coach Al Albert, Asst. Coach Steve Shaw, Paul Grafer. Not Pictured – Asst. Coach Seth Roland.

In 1993, the Tribe accomplished something that no other W&M team had done: return to the NCAA tournament in consecutive years. Running out to a 12-1-1 start and a top-10 national ranking, it faded a bit toward the end of the season but still managed the at-large bid. Its reward was a trip to powerful UVA at Klockner Stadium. Despite an equalizing goal by freshman Steve Jolley, the Tribe bowed to the eventual champion Cavaliers 2-1. Chris Norris would be voted MVP of the season by his teammates and along with Billy Owens, Paul Grafer, and Jolley was named All-CAA. Owens and Jolley would also be selected for the All–South Atlantic regional team. Below, 1993 captain Guy Cartwright moves forward as teammates Jon Kamara and Chris Norris support.

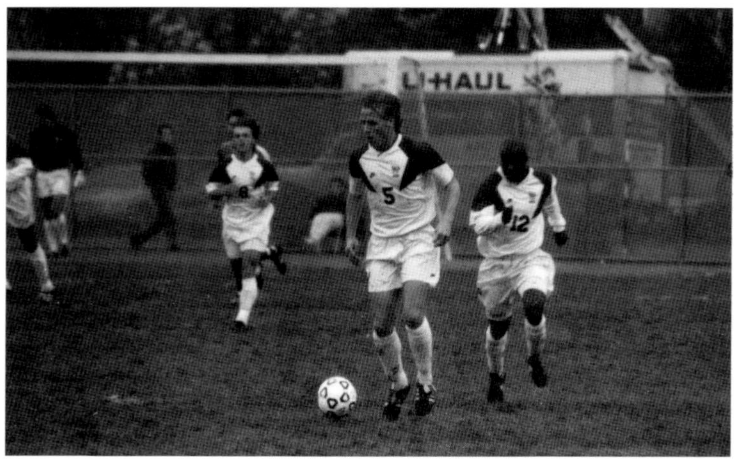

The cover of the 1993 media guide shows fifth-year senior John Metzger, a starter on defense for the Tribe. Metzger had to sit out the 1992 season with a knee injury but then returned to the lineup to anchor the Tribe backline.

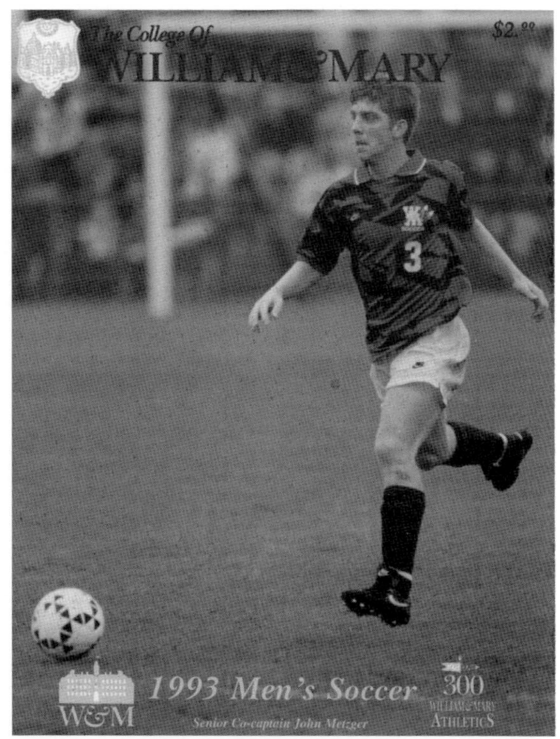

The College Of
WILLIAM & MARY
1993 Men's Soccer
W&M
Senior Co-captain John Metzger
300
ATHLETICS

Chris Scrofani celebrates a goal for the Tribe. Scrofani was a left-footed wide midfielder for the Tribe from 1992 to 1995. He was named second-team All-CAA in 1993. For four years, he was a very consistent goal producer for the Tribe, scoring between four and seven goals each season for a total of 23 goals in his career.

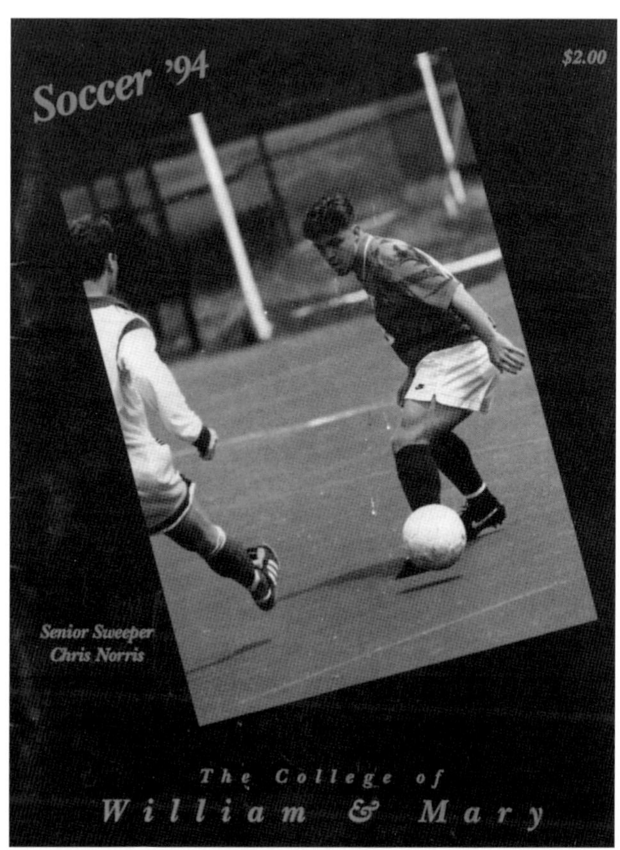

Soccer '94
$2.00
Senior Sweeper
Chris Norris
The College of
William & Mary

The cover of the 1994 W&M yearbook featured senior Chris Norris, who is now W&M's fifth head men's soccer coach after serving nine years as an assistant coach. The team completed the regular season and league playoffs that year at 18-3-1 but was snubbed by the NCAA selection committee and ended its season with a 3-1 loss to JMU at home in the CAA Tournament final. The team had started the season 12-0 before losing to Duke at Busch Field 2-1. Its only losses were Duke, Georgetown, and JMU in the CAA final. Below, Waughn Hughes (right), Wade Barrett (left), and Steve Jolley (center) walk off the field dejectedly at the end of the CAA final still not realizing they would also fail to get an NCAA bid in 1994.

FIRST ROUND • NOV. 18, 1995 • TRANQUILITY PARK • OMAHA, NEB.

William & Mary vs. Creighton

Tribe

Bluejays

1995 William & Mary Results
17-5-0

Date	Opponent (Att.)	Score	Rec.
9/2	**Virginia Tech (4,455)**	**W, 5-1**	**1-0-0**
9/8	**Ohio State (2,417)**	**W, 3-1 (OT)**	**2-0-0**
9/9	**Connecticut (2,574)**	**W, 3-1 (OT)**	**3-0-0**
9/12	* at Va. Commonwealth (500)	L, 0-1	3-1-0
9/15	at College of Charleston (400)	W, 2-1	4-1-0
9/17	at North Carolina (1,100)	L, 1-2	4-2-0
9/22	% vs. Loyola	L, 1-2	4-3-0
9/24	% vs. Adelphi	W, 4-0	5-3-0
9/27	**Georgetown (801)**	**W, 4-0**	**6-3-0**
9/30	*** UNC-Wilmington (1,819)**	**W, 4-0**	**7-3-0**
10/4	*** East Carolina (175)**	**W, 1-0**	**8-3-0**
10/7	* at American (551)	W, 4-1	9-3-0
10/11	at Duke (575)	W, 2-1	10-3-0
10/14	*** George Mason (1,500)**	**W, 4-3**	**11-3-0**
10/18	at North Carolina St. (425)	L, 0-1	11-4-0
10/21	* at James Madison (600)	W, 4-0	12-4-0
10/25	at Howard	W, 3-0	13-4-0
10/28	*** Old Dominion (2,000)**	**L, 1-2**	**13-5-0**
11/4	*** Richmond (2,011)**	**W, 2-0**	**14-5-0**
11/9	$ vs. East Carolina	W, 5-0	15-5-0
11/10	$ vs. American	W, 2-0	16-5-0
11/12	$ vs. George Mason	W, 1-0	17-5-0

% - MetLife Classic at Old Dominion
* - Colonial Athletic Association matches
$ - indicates CAA Tournament at James Madison

1995 Creighton Results
14-2-1

Date	Opponent (Att.)	Score	Rec.
9/2	**#20 Duke (3,120)**	**L, 1-3**	**0-1-0**
9/3	**Northern Illinois (1,182)**	**W, 3-0**	**1-1-0**
9/8	$ vs. Stanford (650)	W, 2-1	2-1-0
9/10	$ at #25 San Francisco	W, 4-3 (OT)	3-1-0
9/15	**#16 Southern Methodist (2,891)**	**L, 1-2**	**3-2-0**
9/17	**Wisconsin-Green Bay (526)**	**W, 6-0**	**4-2-0**
9/23	**Wisconsin (793)**	**W, 2-1**	**5-2-0**
9/24	**New Mexico (702)**	**W, 2-0**	**6-2-0**
9/29	**Missouri-Kansas City (1,727)**	**W, 8-1**	**7-2-0**
10/6	* at Bradley (150)	W, 6-1	8-2-0
10/8	at Marquette (615)	W, 3-0	9-2-0
10/13	* at Evansville (744)	W, 2-1	10-2-0
10/20	* SW Missouri State (810)	W, 3-0	11-2-0
10/22	*** Tulsa (1,262)**	**T, 0-0 (OT)**	**11-2-1**
10/29	*** Drake (1,201)**	**W, 1-0**	**12-2-1**
11/3	% vs. SW Missouri State	W, 5-2	13-2-1
11/5	% at Evansville	W, 2-1	14-2-1

HOME MATCHES IN BOLD
$ - MetLife Classic at San Francisco
• - MVC regular-season matches
% - MVC Tournament matches at Evansville, Ind.

The 1995 NCAA first-round playoff game versus Creighton was one of the most exciting games in program history. Despite a strong team and record, W&M was sent to Omaha for its first-round match. Creighton led 1-0 late in the game when the Tribe was awarded a corner. Goalkeeper Paul Grafer went up into the Creighton box, where all 11 Bluejays defended. The ball bounced off his thigh to Steve Jolley, who pounded it into the net. In overtime, just before going to penalties, Waughn Hughes was put through by Dave McGowan and scored to send the Tribe to the next round. The Tribe flew home and then came back days later to Madison, Wisconsin, to face the Badgers in the second round. It lost in overtime, and Wisconsin went on to win the national title.

The 1996 team reached the quarterfinals of the NCAA tournament, losing in overtime to the eventual champions, St. John's, at the ODU Soccer Stadium. Shown from left to right are (first row) John Coffin, Nelson Warley, Cam Mayer, Andy Crapol, Garrett Chittum, Matt Hansen, Gabe Valencia, Shawn Rice, Luke Bockelmann, and Dan Zickefoose; (second row) Joe Pombriant, Scott Powers, Wade Barrett, Jeff Dominguez, Des McCarthy, Dave McGowan, Andy Pillari, Rob Bryden, Adin Brown, and Dan Flaherty; (third row) coach Seth Roland, coach Chris Scrofani, manager Chris Heishman, Waughn Hughes, Steve Jolley, Michelle Freeman, Heather Fedi, Amity Rubeor, Greg Westfall, Josh Quinter, Mike Botta, coach Oliver Weiss, coach Chris Norris, and coach Al Albert. To reach the third round, they had to come from behind to beat Army 3-1 in the opening round at ODU and the Maryland Terps in College Park 3-0 on a very soggy pitch. Waughn Hughes led the team in scoring with 24 goals, and true freshman Adin Brown took over the goalkeeping duties four games into the season to register eight shutouts.

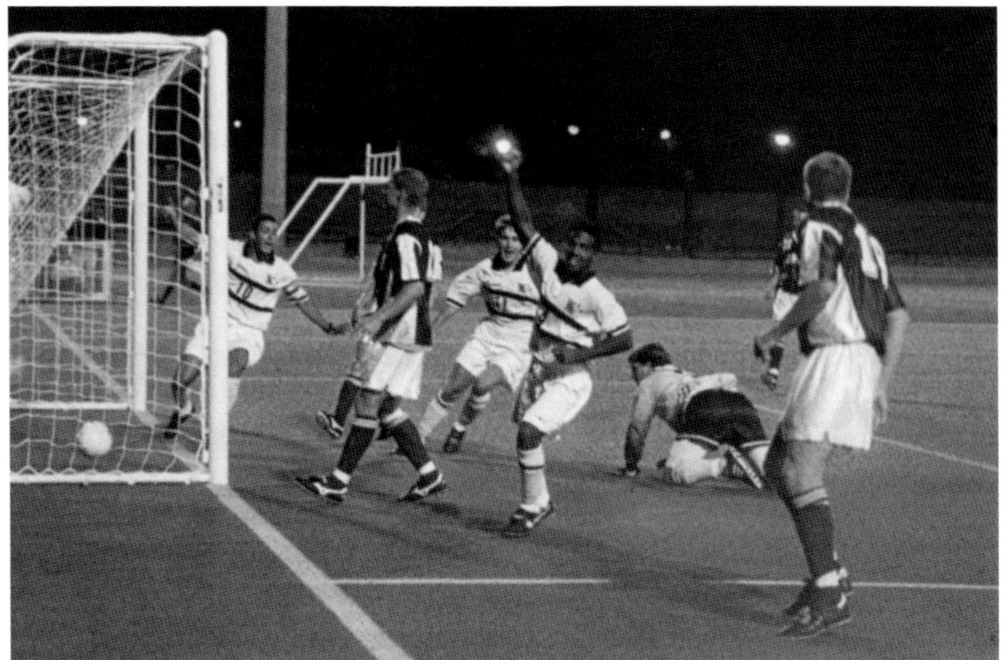

Three of the key players of the 1996 team—from left to right, Steve Jolley, Josh Quinter, and Waughn Hughes—celebrate a goal over JMU in the 3-0 regular season game at Busch Field. The Tribe would defeat JMU again that year in Harrisonburg for the CAA title and go on to log a 20-3-1 record, the most wins in school history.

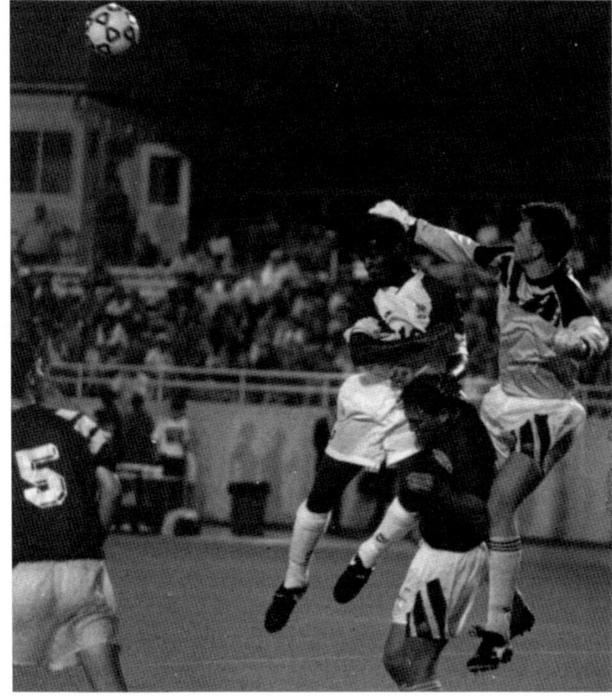

Waughn Hughes challenges for a ball in the air at Busch Field. Although he did not often score goals with his head, Waughn had a tremendous vertical leap. In his senior year, he led the nation in points scored and scored 11 game-winning goals for the Tribe in its 20-win season.

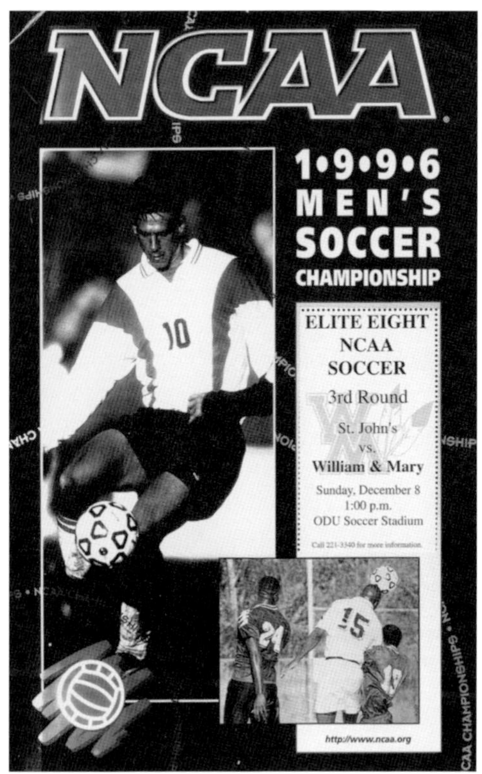

This poster was used to promote the NCAA quarterfinal match in 1996 between the Tribe and St. John's. The Red Storm won and went on to win the national title the next weekend in Richmond. It was the second time the Tribe had made it to the Elite Eight. The game was played at ODU, because the NCAA would not send the game to the Astroturf at Busch Field.

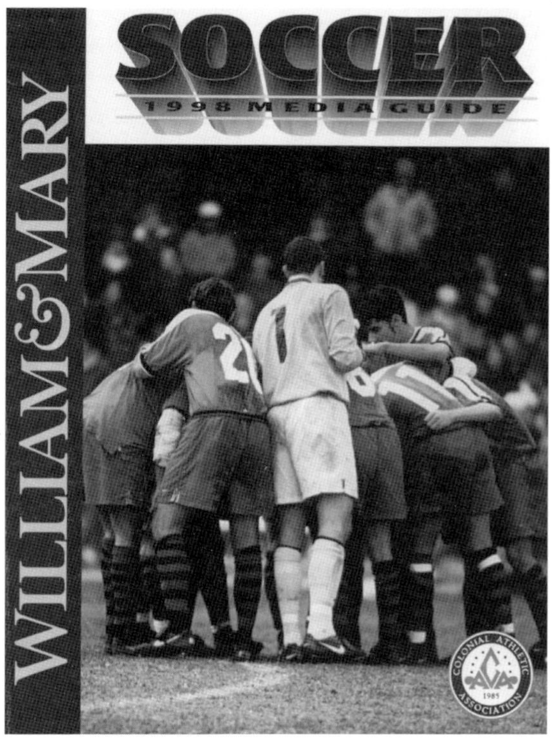

The cover of the 1998 yearbook shows the Tribe in its pregame huddle before the NCAA game with American University in 1997. The Tribe made it back to the NCAA tournament behind All-Americans Wade Barrett and Adin Brown. Despite taking a 1-0 lead against American in overtime (before the golden goal rule was implemented), it lost the NCAA game 2-1. Senior Dave McGowan scored the Tribe's goal.

Dave McGowan moves past an Army defender during the NCAA first-round match in 1996 at the ODU Soccer Stadium. McGowan was an outstanding wide midfielder and forward who also had a very long throw. He used this ability several times to combine with Waughn Hughes, including important goals against Creighton in 1995 and UNC in 1996.

The 1998 Tribe soccer squad started out 4-0, including an exciting overtime win away at Penn State. Despite losing both games in its own tournament at Busch Field, it rallied later in the season to beat Rutgers and Maryland. As a result, it was awarded an at-large bid to the NCAA tournament, even after losing in the CAA final to Richmond in overtime. Luke Bockelmann was the leading scorer with nine goals and four assists. Probably the most dramatic moment of the season came in the first-round NCAA game versus USF. Leading most of the match, W&M was gutted when USF tied the game with less than three minutes to go in regulation. Hanging tough, the Tribe took the game into overtime, when Andy Pillari stripped a Bulls defender and stuck away the winner. The season would end the following week with a 1-0 loss at Clemson.

The Tribe won the CAA title in 1999, compiling a 14-7-3 season record. Its big wins were a 4-1 victory over South Carolina and a 1-0 win at UVA. In the CAA final against VCU, it jumped out to a 3-0 lead by halftime and held on to win 4-2. In the NCAA first round, it dropped a 1-0 game at Penn State.

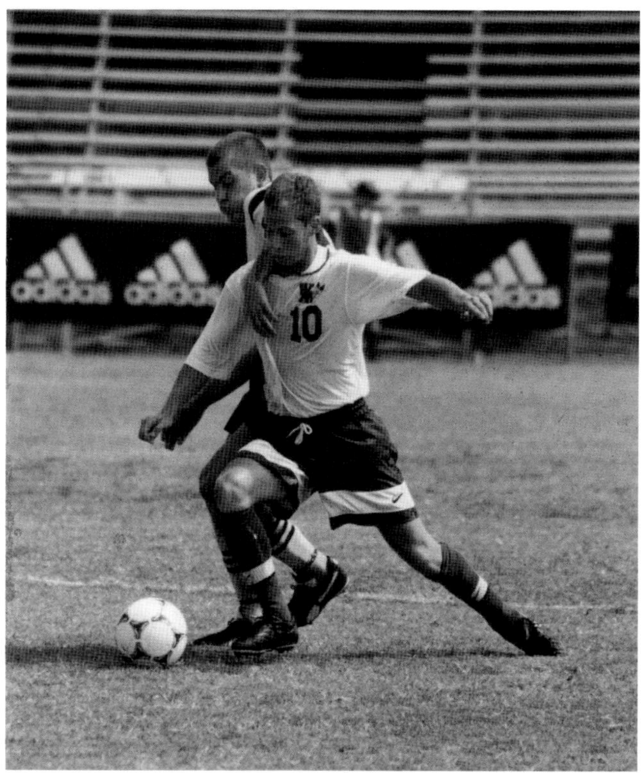

Brian Hinkey transferred to W&M in 1997 after an outstanding freshman year at Vanderbilt, where he was one of the country's leaders in assists. Brian was a key player in the Tribe's run to the NCAA tournament the next three seasons. He finished with 23 assists in three seasons and is presently ninth on the all-time career-assist list for the Tribe.

In 2000, the Tribe won the CAA again with one of the most dominating performances in league history. Back at the Virginia Beach Sportsplex, the team beat its three opponents by combined scores of 14-0 behind a solid defense and goalkeeper Trevor Upton. Justin Smiley was named MVP of the tournament. It lost 3-2 in overtime in the first round of the NCAA tournament to a top-ranked UNC team.

Kevin Knott was the MVP of the 2000 season. His 15 assists that year from his left back position are the second highest all-time season mark in school history. They resulted from a combination of taking corners and surging forward from his left back position. Kevin was also tapped for Phi Beta Kappa and is presently a doctoral candidate in physics at Stanford.

The team relaxes between games at the Florida International University tournament in late October 2000. W&M won the event, beating Butler 5-2 and then FIU 1-0 in the final. After losing its last regular-season match against VCU a week later, the Tribe rolled through the CAA tournament.

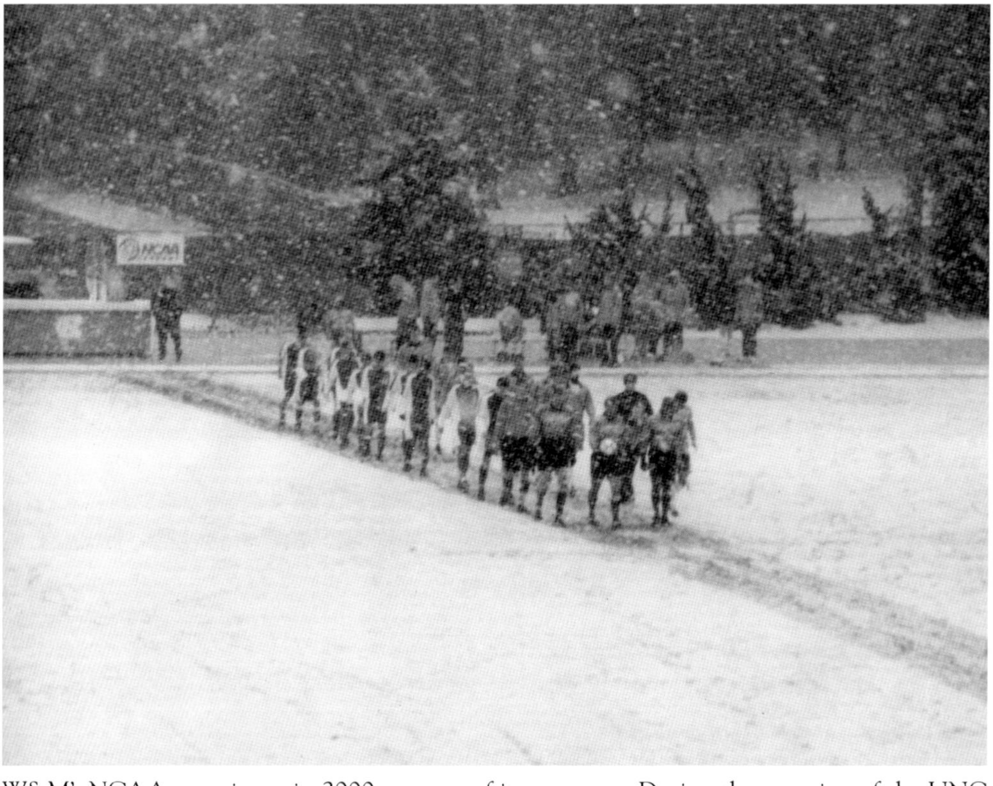

W&M's NCAA experience in 2000 was one of its strangest. During the morning of the UNC game in Chapel Hill, it began to snow as the team arrived at the stadium. By game time, the field was completely covered by a freak snowstorm. Throughout the match, there was 1–2 inches of snow on the ground, changing the game into a match of field position rather than ball possession. Despite taking a 2-0 lead, W&M lost 3-2 in overtime to end its magical late-season run.

From left to right, Doug Henry, Carlos Garcia, and Phil Hucles celebrate a goal during the 2001 season. The following year, these three would all play key roles in the 2002 team's run to the NCAA final 16. Henry scored the first goal versus Duke in the NCAA first-round match, and Hucles and Garcia were a consistently dangerous one-two punch from 2000 to 2002

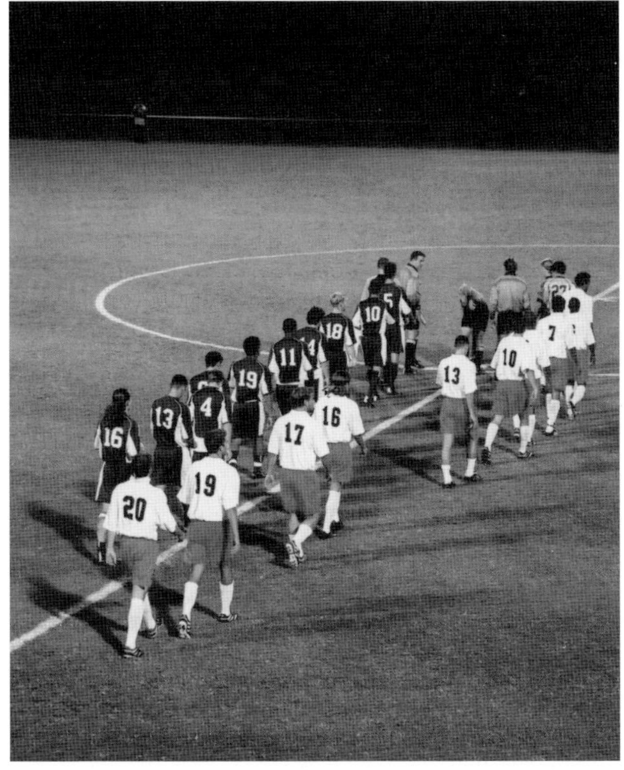

W&M walks out for a game in 2001 at Klockner Field at UVA. Although it would lose this one 0-1 on a penalty call in the waning moments of the game, the Tribe had UVA's number during this period, racking up a record of 3-1-1 versus the Cavaliers from 1999 to 2002. The teams have not played since the NCAA match in 2002, when the Tribe tied in Charlottesville and advanced on penalties.

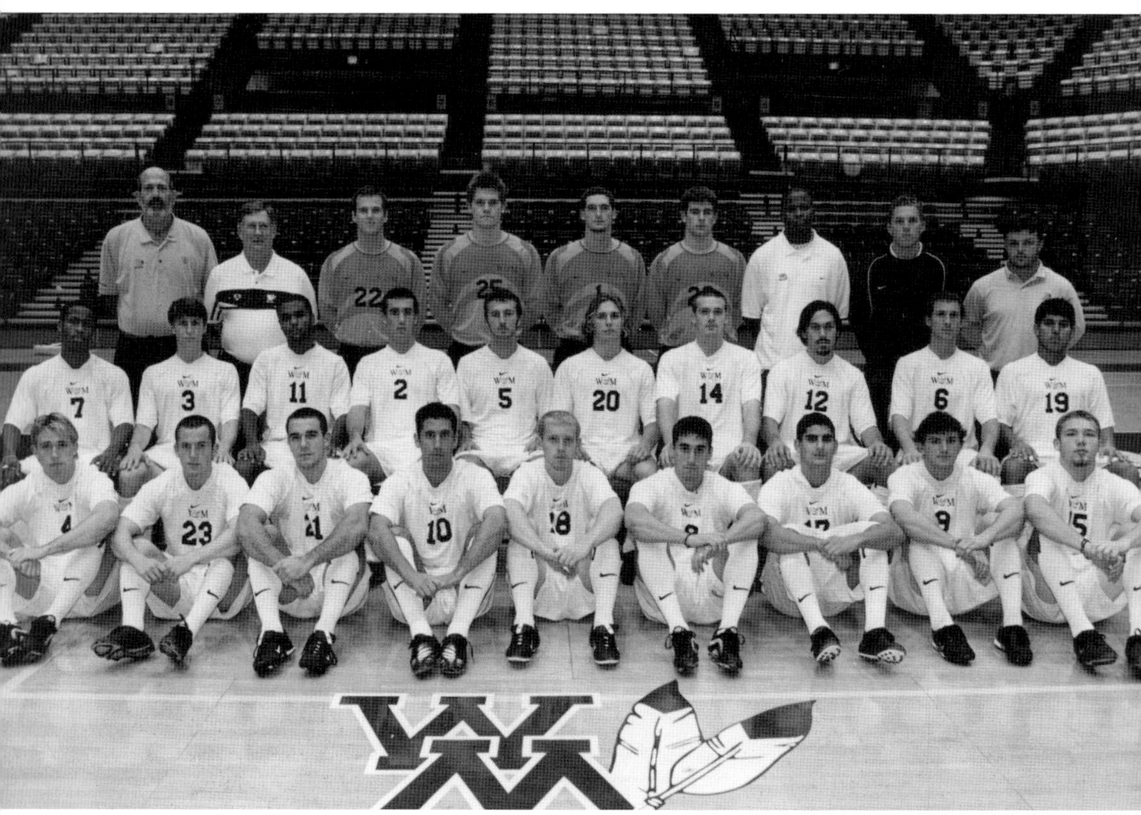

Despite a disappointing season-opening home loss to Appalachian State, the 2002 Tribe squad was 15-8-1 with wins over FIU, UVA, and Loyola. The real story of the season was the NCAA run, beginning with a 2-1 away win at Duke. The goals were scored by midfielders Doug Henry and Ralph Bean. The victory sent the Tribe to Charlottesville for a second-round battle with the Cavaliers. W&M had to beat a strong UVA squad it had beaten earlier in the season. UVA's Alecko Eskandarian scored for the home team in the first half, but the Tribe equalized late in the second and advanced on penalties. In the round of 16, it was again on the road and lost an overtime game to Penn State on a frozen field in State College. It was only the fourth time in school history the team had made it to the NCAA final 16.

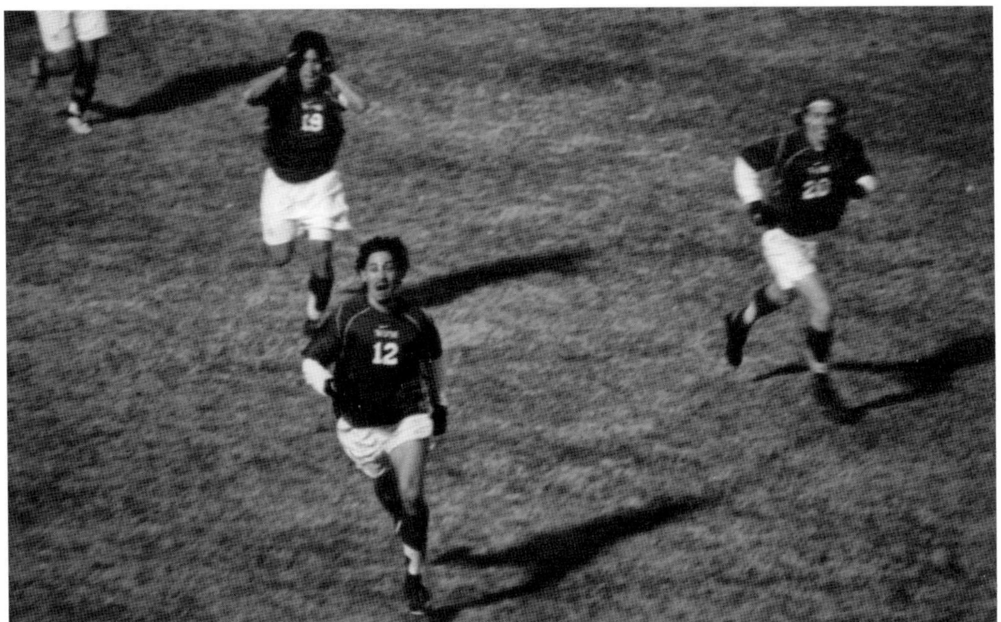

Graham Albert comes to the touchline to celebrate the biggest goal of his career, the tying goal versus UVA in the second round of the NCAA tournament in 2002. Brian Hinkle and Carlos Garcia help with the celebration. Albert would make All-CAA and All–South Atlantic in 2003.

Shown from left to right are Chuck Connelly, Chris Norris, and Tom Duffy, the assistants in 2002 and currently the nucleus of the coaching staff. Connelly was an outstanding goalkeeper at ODU, Norris played at W&M, and Duffy came to Williamsburg after a career as a high school coach in Oneonta, New York, an assistant at Hartwick College, and a head coach at Oneonta State University.

The 2008 team finally got W&M back into the NCAA tournament with an 11-7-3 record. For the first time since 1992, a home game in the NCAA tournament was sent to Williamsburg. The Tribe defeated Big South champion Winthrop by a score of 3-1. Faced with top-seeded Wake Forest in the second round, it battled the Demon Deacons to a 1-0 overtime loss. Doug McBride (left), a senior captain, was the first player since Adin Brown to repeat as team MVP. Only Brown, McBride, and Paul Grafer have accomplished this feat.

Nathan Belcher walked on to the W&M team as a junior in 2006 and was a squad member for three years. Although he scored only four goals in his career, his uplifting presence on the team was so influential that he is the only two-time winner of the Crapol Award (formerly the Coaches' Award) in the history of the program.

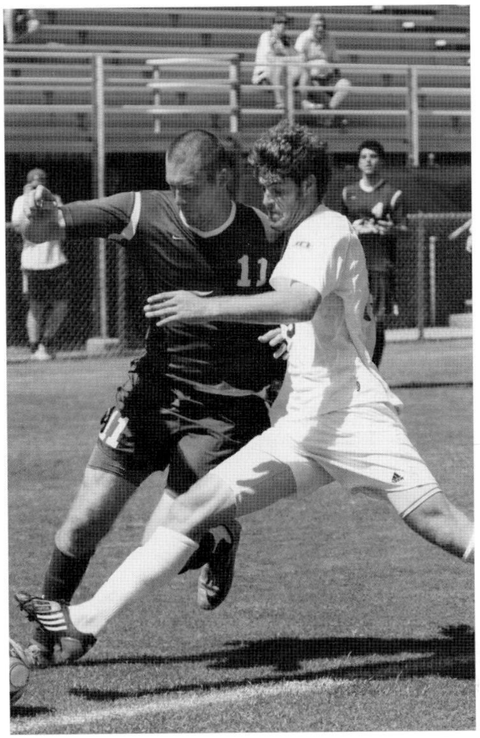

Nat Baako was the first Tribe player to come to Tribe soccer directly from the continent of Africa. George Attoh of Liberia played briefly for W&M in the 1970s, and Jon Kamara moved to Indianapolis as a youth, but Baako had never left his homeland of Ghana prior to coming to Williamsburg in the fall of 2007. As a sophomore and junior, he was named first-team all-CAA.

The NCAA first round game at Albert-Daly Field in 2008 was played on a chilly night in front of 542 fans. Before most of them were seated, Andrew Hoxie had scored the first of three first-half goals to lead the Tribe to a surprisingly easy 3-1 victory. Hoxie also scored the second goal at 9:32 to become the third W&M player to score two goals in an NCAA game and the first to do it in less than a 10-minute span. Below, the team celebrates one of Hoxie's goals.

7

Women's Soccer in Williamsburg

Although women's soccer was slower to develop in the greater Williamsburg area and at W&M, it soon made up for lost time, spurred on by Title IX legislation in the early 1980s.

The first women's soccer club emerged in the late 1970s, and by 1981, it was a varsity sport. Physical education professor John Charles was the first coach from 1981 to 1986; in 1982, he was joined by assistant coach John Daly, who was also assisting Al Albert with the men's team. By 1986, Daly was a full-time assistant with the women, and in 1987, he took over the program.

Youth soccer for girls had become extremely developed in Northern Virginia, and the high school teams benefited from this growth. Three women from Fairfax County came to W&M in 1984 without any scholarship money and all became All-Americans. Megan McCarthy was named National Player of the Year her senior year, and Julie Cunningham Shackford and Jill Ellis also went on to become All-Americans and head college coaches at Princeton and UCLA respectively. This was the beginning of the juggernaut of W&M women's soccer.

Under Daly, the program has become one of the top college programs in the country with a consecutive winning season streak of 29 seasons. Its total of 23 NCAA bids is third most in NCAA history for Division I women's teams. The program has won nine CAA championships and has produced 13 All-Americans and 10 CAA Players of the Year. Daly himself has been CAA Coach of the Year four times, Regional Coach of the Year six times, and has produced five players who have played professionally. In 2008, he passed the 300-win mark, only the ninth coach in NCAA Division I women's soccer to achieve this mark.

The era of women's varsity soccer began in the 1980s, but here is a picture of a women's soccer club on campus around 1928, courtesy of the Martha Barksdale Archives at Swem Library. Barksdale was the legendary professor of physical education for women at the college, and this is clearly a large soccer club, which probably played intramural matches.

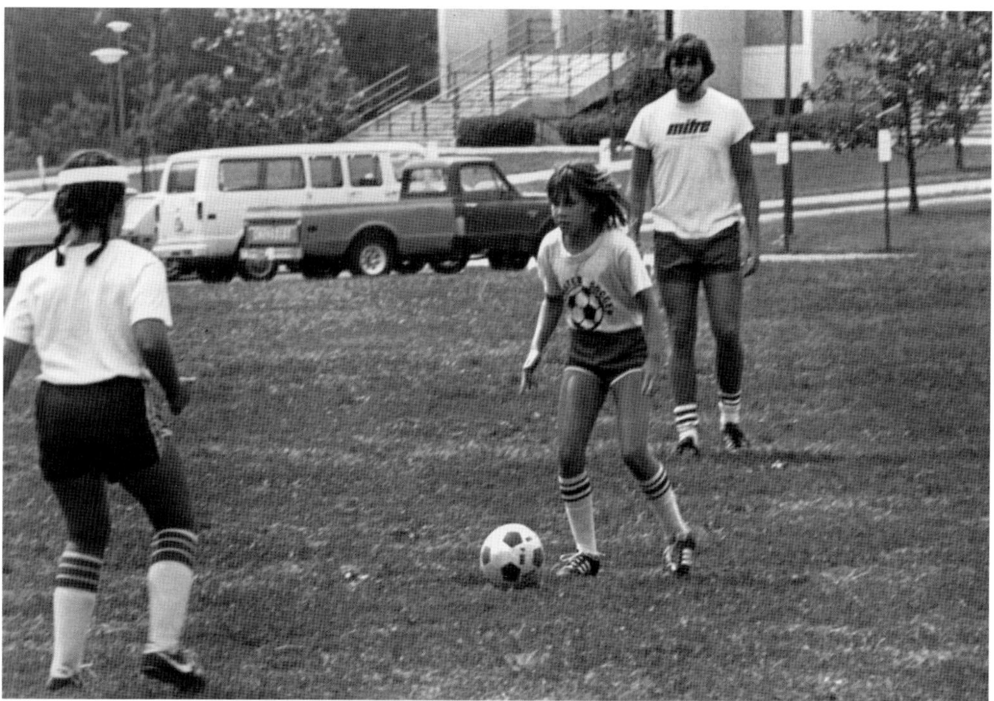

Prior to the establishment of the women's varsity soccer team at W&M, the Tidewater Soccer Camp (TSC) offered a girls-only camp week as part of its program. Here Kelly Alford watches his younger group play on the Yates Field across from W&M Hall. All-American Julie Cunningham was a camper at TSC prior to coming to W&M.

John Charles (middle) and John Daly (right) talk to the team at halftime of a game at Central Florida in 1984. At that time, the Knights were a big name in women's college soccer, led by Hall of Famer Michelle Akers. Akers would score two goals in this game, and the Tribe would lose 3-1. However, the team would go on to be the first women's soccer team in school history to play in the NCAA tournament.

John Charles was the original W&M women's coach and the only individual besides John Daly to lead the Tribe women. His six-year coaching record from 1981 to 1986 was 63-32-13, and his 1984, 1985, and 1986 teams advanced to the NCAA tournament. In 1983, he was named Regional Coach of the Year. Charles remains as a faculty member at W&M.

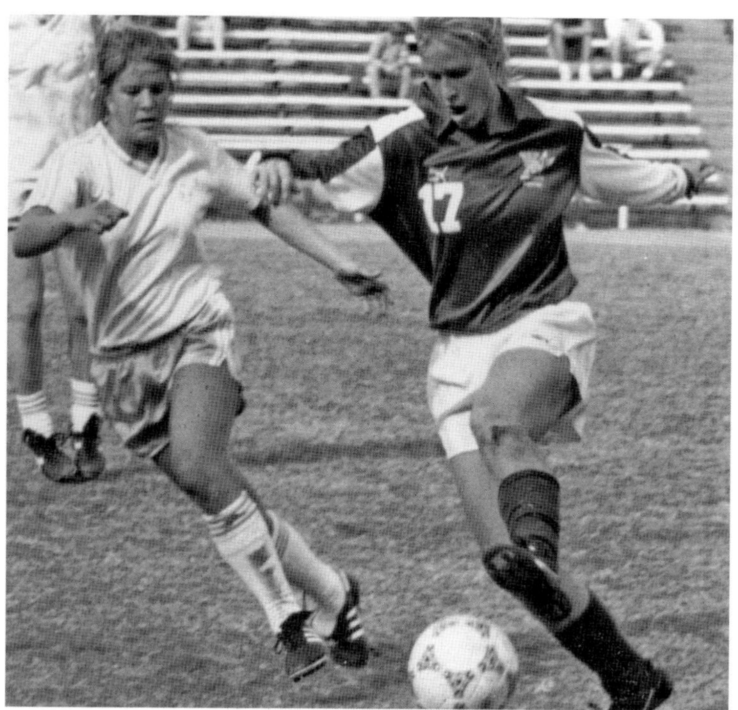

Megan McCarthy, the first National Player of the Year for the Tribe, was a three-time All-American sweeper for the Tribe from 1985 to 1987. She also played over 30 times for the full U.S. National Team but tore her ACL before she was able to compete in the Women's World Cup. Here she is in action against UNC's Marcia McDermott, current president of the NSCAA.

Julie Cunningham looks to serve left-footed versus George Washington. Julie was a three-time All-American midfielder for the Tribe from 1985 to 1987 and now is the head women's soccer coach at Princeton. She represented the East in the 1985 Sports Festival.

The 1987 team, John Daly's first as a head coach, was one of his most special at W&M. Shown from left to right are (first row) Kathie Stough, Diane Wright, Kristen Jesulaitis, Joyce Flood, Jen Tepper, and Margie Vaughn; (second row) Jennifer Volgenau, Sandra Gaskill, Laura Absalom, Gail Brophy, Kathy Carter, Amy McDowell, Colleen Corwell, Stacy Zeman, and Jennifer Johns; (third row) trainer Karen Patterson, Debbie Matson, Julie Cunningham, Megan McCarthy, coach John Daly, coach April Heinrichs, Holly Barrett, Nancy Reinisch, Jill Ellis, and Robin Lotze. Besides the three 1987 All-Americans (Cunningham, Ellis, and McCarthy), there were two future All-Americans, Sandra Gaskill and Robin Lotze. There was also a young goalkeeper, Kathy Carter, who is now the executive vice president of Soccer United Marketing. Daly's assistant that year was April Heinrichs, a great player in her own right who later became the U.S. Women's National Team coach. The team made it to the NCAA quarterfinals, losing to UNC 2-0 in Chapel Hill. It had previously tied UNC in the WAGS (Washington Area Girls Soccer League) final and won the tournament title on penalty kicks. W&M's final record was 10-7-3.

Jill Ellis, an All-American from the 1987 team, is now the head women's soccer coach at UCLA. Ellis was an elegant forward for the Tribe and often drew the main attention of opposing defenses. She was the assistant for the gold-medal-winning U.S. Women's National Team in the 2008 Beijing Olympics. In January 2010, Jill was the head coach for the U.S. U-20 Women's National Team, which qualified for the world championships.

Natalie Neaton, one of two National Players of the Year that Tribe soccer has produced, is the all-time goal scorer for W&M women's soccer. In her career, she averaged over 20 goals a season for a total of 81 goals. Her biggest production was 28 goals in 1994, when she led the Tribe back to the Elite Eight, losing at Notre Dame 2-1. Natalie was also a four-time All-American from 1992 to 1995.

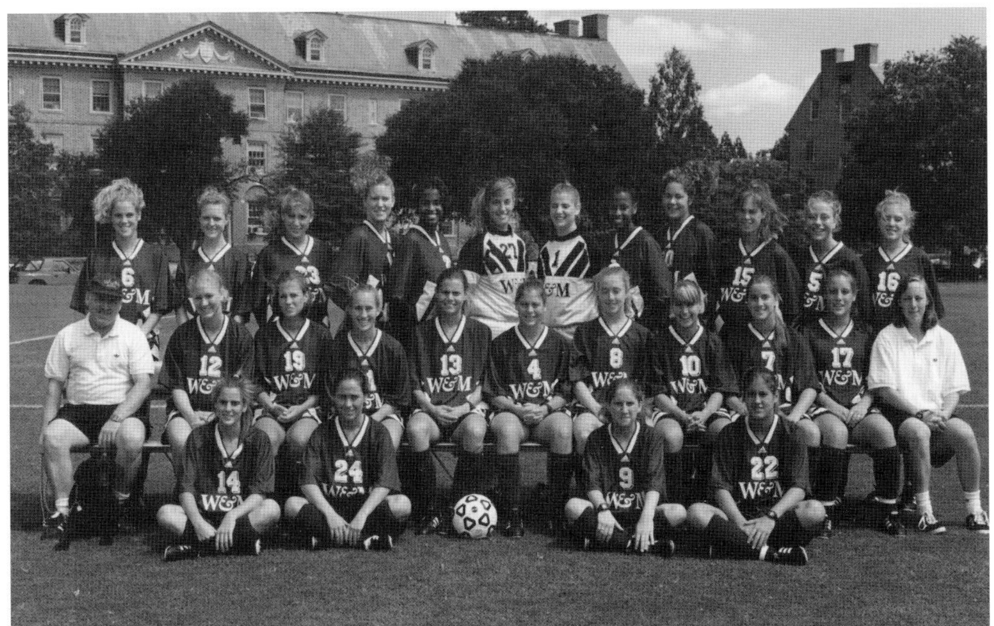

In 1994, W&M won the league championship in the first year of CAA women's soccer. After an outstanding regular season in which it won 11 straight games, the Tribe knocked off Washington State 4-0 in the first round of the NCAA tournament. Its season ended by losing to Notre Dame 2-1.

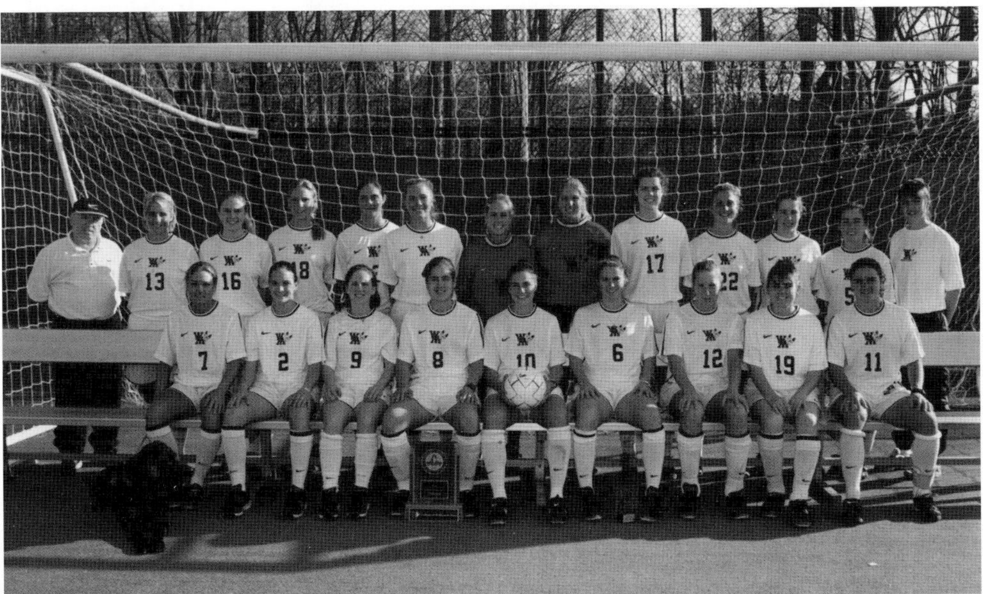

The 1997 team brought another CAA championship team to W&M. It went on to the Elite Eight again, winning away at Penn State and UVA to do so. Its season ended in Storrs, Connecticut, when it lost to a strong UConn squad. Ann Cook and Missy Wycinsky were All-Americans, and Cook was CAA Player of the Year.

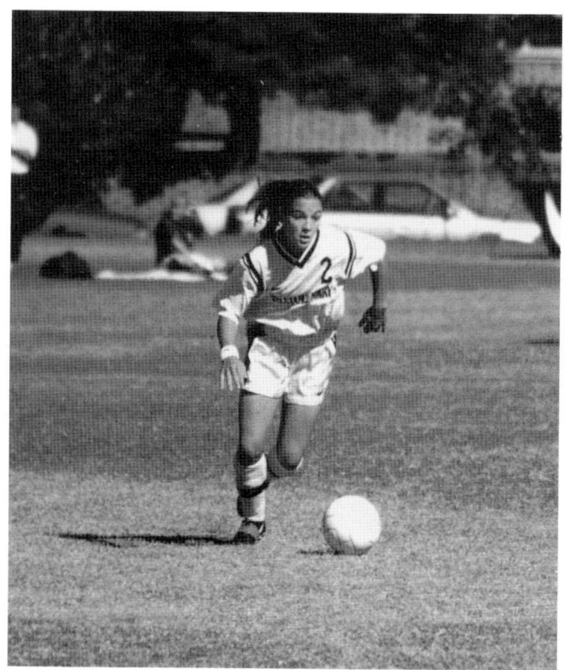

Although never a National Player of the Year, Missy Wycinsky was a three-time All-American from 1997 to 1999 and is the all-time points leader for the W&M women's program. Her 75 career goal total is second to Neaton's, but she had 52 assists to go with it for a total of 202 points.

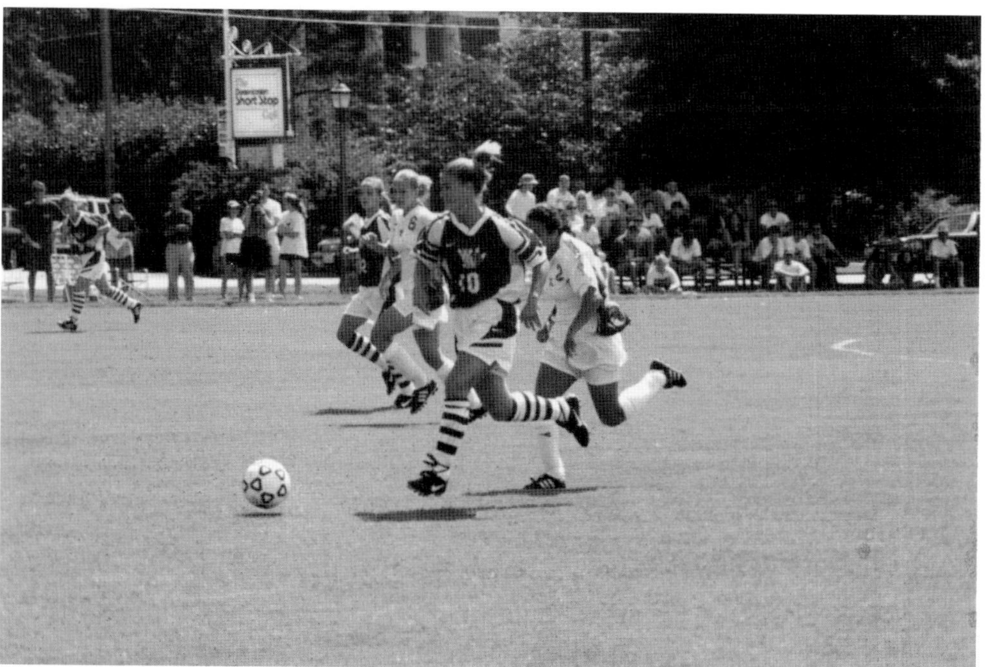

Ann Cook was another three-time All-American for the Tribe in 1993, 1995, and 1997. She is third all-time in career points behind Wycinsky and Neaton and is the only midfield player in the top 10 on that list. She was drafted in the first round of the Women's United Soccer Association (WUSA) draft in 2001 and played in the league for three years. She now is an assistant coach at Penn State for another former W&M star, Erica Walsh.

The 2006 team was unique. Despite getting bounced out of the first round of the NCAA tournament by a Navy squad on penalty kicks, it only lost one game. Its final record was 16-1-4. There were no All-Americans during this season, but two sophomores from the team, Dani Collins and Claire Zimmeck, would go on to become two-time All-Americans.

Kathy Carter was goalkeeper for the Tribe from 1987 to 1990. After her playing career, she went into sports marketing and is presently the executive vice president for Soccer United Marketing, the marketing arm of the U.S. national teams and Major League Soccer. Kathy also served as the first four-year chairperson of the Friends of Women's Soccer, the group that raises funds to support the Tribe women's program.

One must end the chapter on the incredible success of the W&M women's program with the driving force behind the program. In 2008, John Daly became only the fourth women's soccer coach in NCAA Division I history to win 300 games at the same school. "J. D." has coached 13 Tribe All-Americans and two National Players of the Year. His teams have won nine CAA Championships and been to the NCAA tournament 20 of the 23 years he has coached the team. The Tribe women have not had a losing season in the 29 years Daly has been associated with them as an assistant or the head coach. Their consecutive winning season string is only topped by two schools, UNC and UConn.

8

Honor Roll

Through the past 45 years, there have been many honors awarded to W&M players. From Gary King (All–Southern Conference in 1965) to 2009's honorees, W&M has always been well represented on state, league, regional, and national teams.

Prior to the early 1980s, W&M played men's soccer as a member of the Southern Conference (SC). In 1976, it shared the conference title with a strong Appalachian State team, but in general, it did not have a lot of success in that league in soccer. Davidson, Furman, and Appalachian State dominated SC soccer in the 1970s and 1980s.

Gradually W&M moved into athletic alliances with schools in Virginia and the northeast as a member of the ECAC South division. In 1970s, there were ECAC playoff matches with Rider, Lehigh, LaSalle, and Loyola. In 1983, W&M began to participate in the ECAC South, which officially changed its name to the Colonial Athletic Association in 1985.

For over a quarter of a century, W&M soccer has dominated the CAA, winning more championships (six) than any other school. Of the 25 players chosen for the silver anniversary squad, five were from W&M. Adin Brown, the three-time all-American, was the lone goalkeeper chosen. MLS veterans Wade Barrett and Steve Jolley join all-time scoring leader Waughn Hughes and 1980s star Jon Tuttle to complete the Tribe contingent.

Through the years, W&M's biggest CAA rivals continue to be JMU, ODU, VCU, and George Mason. These rivalries have defined the W&M soccer program over the last 20 years and have made the CAA one of the strongest college soccer leagues in the country. Besides W&M's two appearances in the final eight, VCU and JMU have each made it to that stage of the NCAA Division I championships.

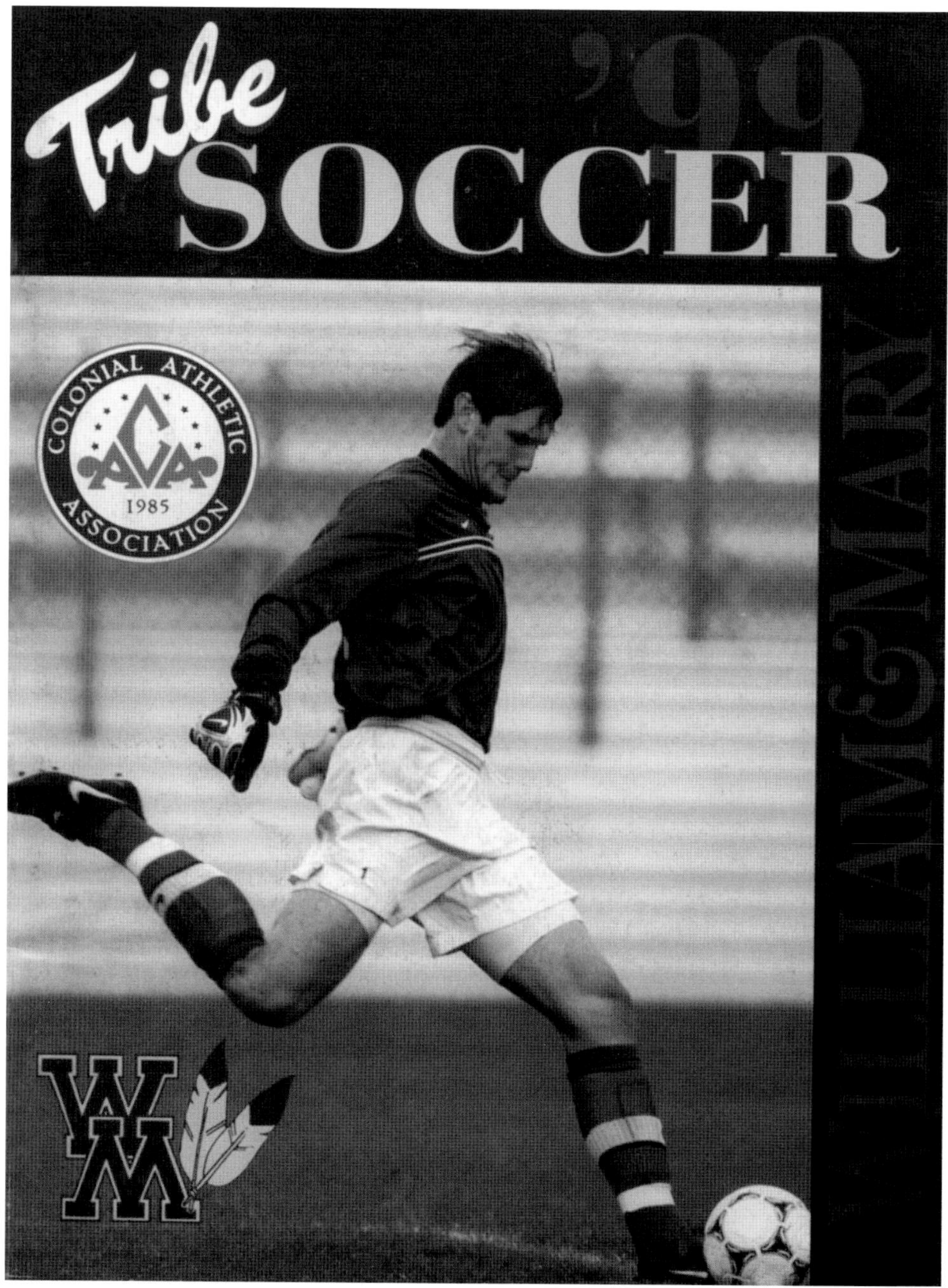

The cover of the 1999 yearbook depicts Adin Brown, a three-time All-American, under-23 national team player, and professional goalkeeper. He followed in the footsteps of his father, Adin Sr., who was a standout of the W&M football team in the 1960s. Adin Jr. holds the Tribe career record for most saves and shutouts. Brown has played professional soccer since leaving Williamsburg. He led the New England Revolution to the MLS Cup in 2002 and has played since then in the top division in Norway. Following on the path of Scott Budnick and Paul Grafer, he was the third goalkeeper from W&M to play in the MLS.

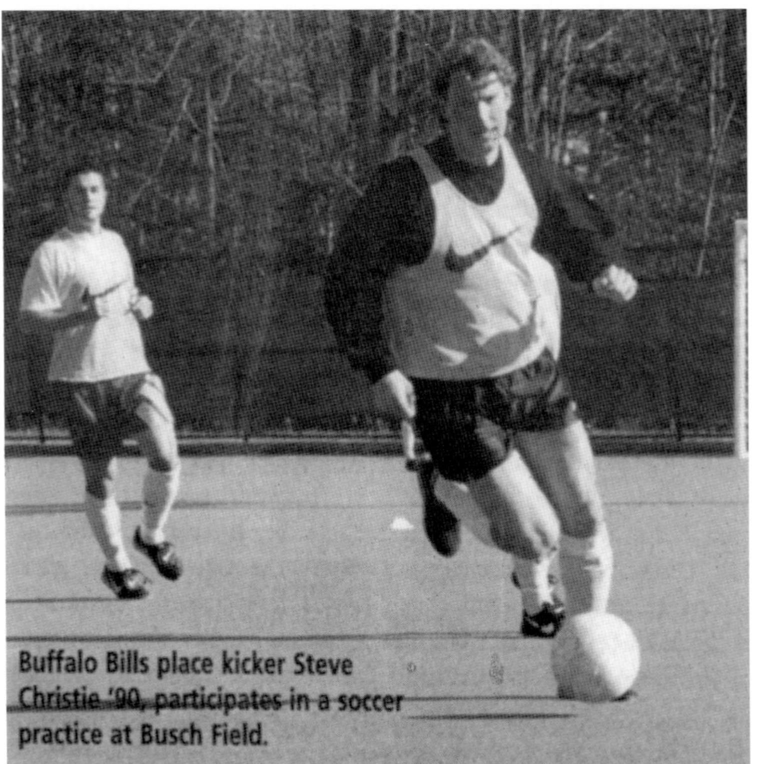

Buffalo Bills place kicker Steve Christie '90, participates in a soccer practice at Busch Field.

Professional football kicker Steve Christie is pictured here practicing with the team as an assistant coach in 1997 and kicking for the W&M football team. In the background of the soccer picture is Wade Barrett. Christie was discovered for W&M by former All-American soccer player and Tribe football kicker Bill Watson playing for a club soccer team in Canada. Watson called Coach Albert and a tape was sent to the football staff. Christie was offered a scholarship and the rest is history, as he was the greatest kicker in Tribe football history and also for the Buffalo Bills. At heart, Christie is a soccer fan—Canada, Scotland, but foremost Glasgow Celtic. He still holds the record for the longest field goal in Super Bowl history, a 54-yarder against Dallas in Super Bowl XXVIII.

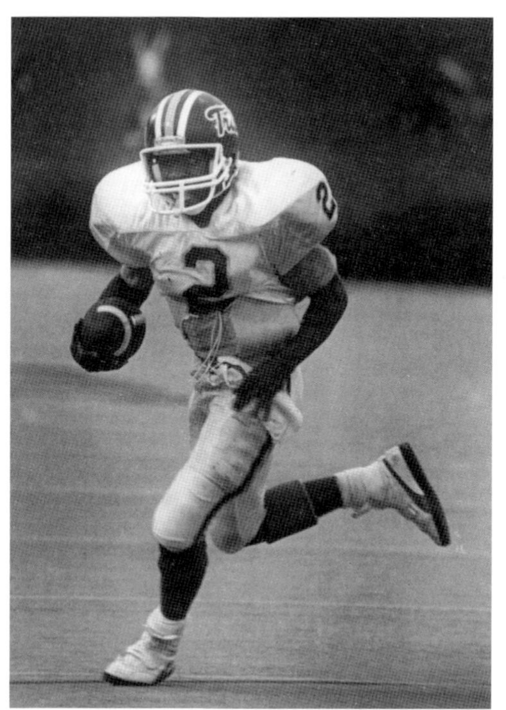

Two other great athletes who played spring soccer for the Tribe but were never able to play in a fall match were Michael Clemons and Curtis Pride. Clemons was an All-American halfback for W&M, and after a professional career in the NFL and Canadian football, he is now general manager for the Toronto Argonauts. Pride was a high school All-America soccer star who played basketball at W&M. He finished a long career with various teams in Major League Baseball and is presently head baseball coach at Gallaudet. Ninety-five percent deaf, Pride received the 2008 Yeagley Award from the NSCAA, given to a former college soccer player who has overcome adversity. One can only imagine if Christie, Clemons, and Pride had ever been able to play for a fall Tribe soccer squad in the late 1980s how good that team could have been.

Steve Jolley controls the ball in front of a big crowd at Busch Field in 1994. Jolley went on to a 10-year career in MLS for Los Angeles, New York, and Dallas and played in an MLS final in 1999 for the Galaxy. He received the league's Humanitarian of the Year Award in 2002 for his charitable endeavors. Jolley currently holds the position of director of sports marketing for SMU athletics.

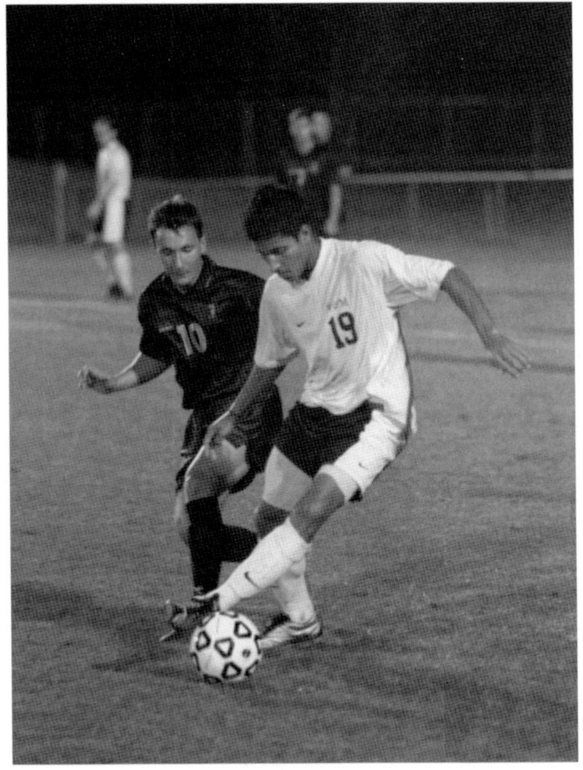

Carlos Garcia screens the ball for the Tribe. Garcia was a four-year starting forward for W&M and is third in all-time goals scored with 45 and second in points with 121. After his career at W&M, he had stints in outdoor professional soccer before settling in with the indoor Baltimore Blast. He has three championship rings with the Blast and also works for First Mariner Bank in Baltimore.

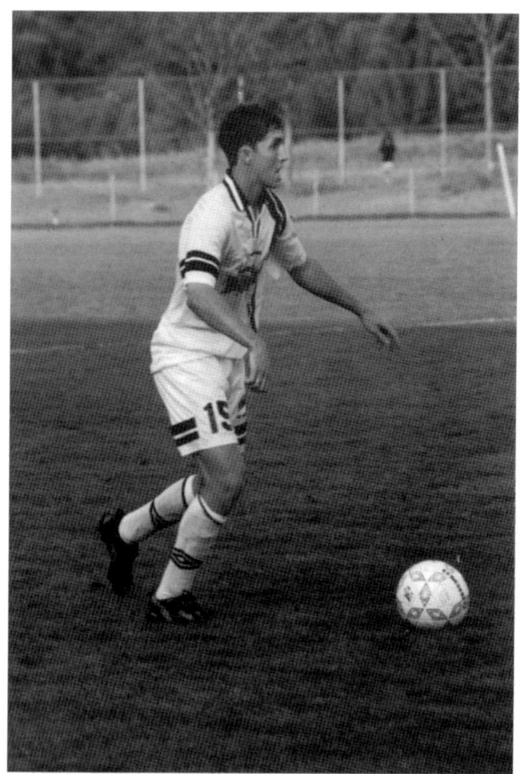

Jeff "Nacho" Dominguez holds the record for most appearances by an individual in NCAA tournament games (8). As a freshman, he played regularly for the team that went to the Elite Eight and then for three subsequent teams that made it to the "show." He finished his career as a pro in Germany for BV Cloppenberg in the Regionaliga and Oberliga after a journeyman career in the USL in this country.

Rich Miranda moves forward at Cary Field. Miranda began his career as one of the best left backs in school history, but an ACL injury hampered his career. He later was an assistant at Richmond, W&M, and Navy before taking over as head coach at the Naval Academy from 2006 to 2008. He is now a tenured instructor of physical education at the Naval Academy.

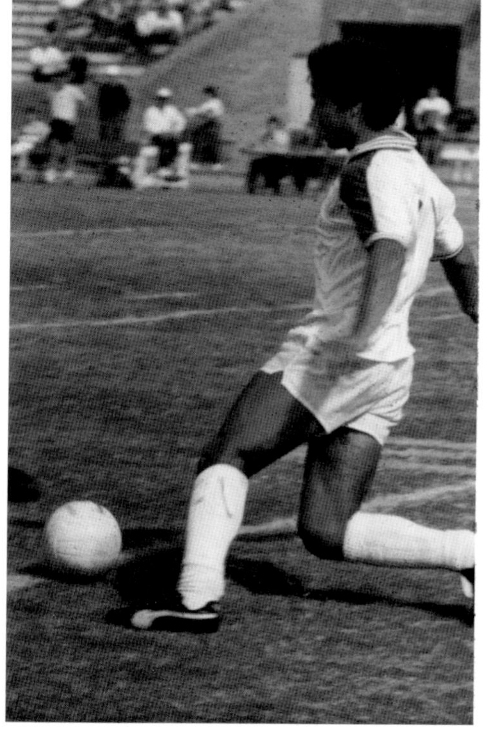

Assistant Coach
Steve
Shaw

Steve Shaw enters his sixth year as the top assistant on the Tribe coaching staff. Until January of '95, Shaw also coached at nearby Lafayette High School, enjoying remarkable success. In 1994 he was named District, Regional and State Coach of the Year after leading Lafayette to the regional title and a semifinal finish in the state tournament.

Shaw sports a career record of 162-62-28 in 14 years, including a 45-18-5 slate after four seasons at Lafayette. All told his teams have qualified for the playoffs 10 times, winning five district and three regional championships. Shaw has coached numerous players who have continued to play soccer in the collegiate ranks. Four of his players from Lafayette are currently playing college soccer, including W&M's Scott Powers and David Schifrin.

Prior to coming to Williamsburg, Shaw served as the head coach of boys' soccer at James E. Taylor High in Katy, Texas. In his seven years there, Shaw's teams posted a 93-21-17 record and won district championships the last three seasons. While living in Katy, Shaw, who earned his United States Soccer Federation "B" license in 1986, also served as director of the La Liga Soccer Club and was coach of the La Liga Olympic Development Program team.

Shaw served as head coach at Berea Community High in Berea, KY, from 1978-80, twice leading his squad to the Central Kentucky Soccer League Tournament Championship.

Shaw played collegiate soccer at Morehead State University in Morehead, KY, where he captained the team in 1973, the same year he was nominated for regional All-America honors. From 1974-75, he played for the La Liga Alajuelense Youth Reserve team in Costa Rica. He went on to play for the state champion Kentucky Kickers amateur team.

Married with three children, Shaw holds a master of arts in Spanish and Portuguese from Eastern Kentucky University. Steve earned his undergraduate degree in physical education from Morehead State. Multilingual, he speaks Spanish fluently and has a working knowledge of Portuguese, French and Italian.

Assistant Coach Chris Norris played for the Tribe last season.

Assistant Coach
Seth
Roland

University of Pennsylvania graduate Seth Roland returns for his fourth season as an assistant coach under Al Albert. The 36-year old Roland arrived in Williamsburg four matches into the 1992 season, and helped direct the Tribe to an 17-match unbeaten streak and a NCAA Tournament bid.

Roland began his coaching career at Christopher Newport University, where he revived a stagnant program, taking the Captains to their only NCAA Division III playoffs in 1986 before finishing 10th in the nation with 18 wins.

Following his stint in Newport News, Roland was named head coach at the University of Bridgeport, where he led the Purple Knights to NCAA Division II playoff bids and top-10 finishes in 1988, 1990 and 1991. His career record stands at 125-60-9 in 10 seasons as a head coach.

As a player, Roland competed as a midfielder for the University of Pennsylvania Quakers where he graduated with a B.A. in history and an M.S. in education. He played for the United States in four World Maccabiah Games, leading W&M coach Al Albert's silver medalist squad in scoring in 1981. Roland served as head coach for the 1993 bronze medal team.

Roland also served as the head coach for the regional under-23 men's squad from 1988-94 and coached the East team in five U.S. Olympic Festivals.

Volunteer Assistant
Chris
Norris

Joining the Tribe men's staff in 1995 is former Tribe star Chris Norris. Norris will be making the transition from playing field to sideline after he was the squad's defensive leader and captain last year. In his senior campaign, Norris recorded nine assists and earned All-South Atlantic honors. He was a two-time All-CAA performer during his career and also selected first team all-state in 1994. The team's Most Valuable Player as a junior, Norris received the Coaches' Award in 1992 and earned W&M rookie of the year honors in 1991. Norris also received the team's freshman academic achievement award in 1991.

He graduated in May with a degree in kinesiology.

This page from the 1995 media guide shows the quality of the coaching staff in the mid-1990s. All these assistants, including first-year volunteer undergraduate assistant Chris Norris, have become successful college head coaches. Seth Roland actually had been a successful head coach first, leading Christopher Newport at the Division III level and then Bridgeport at the Division II level. He has since gone on to take Fairleigh Dickinson University to the quarterfinals of the Division I NCAA tournament. Steve Shaw left in 1995 to build the Christopher Newport program into a Division III powerhouse, achieving the school's first No. 1 national ranking in any sport in 2009. Chris Norris, after four years of establishing his team at W&M, broke through into the second round of the NCAA tournament in 2008 and was named that year's W&M Coach of the Year among the school's 23 sports.

Gary King, an all–Southern Conference fullback and the first W&M player ever to receive any all-star recognition, kicks the ball forward during the 1965 season. King was an assistant coach to Joe Agee in the 1967 season.

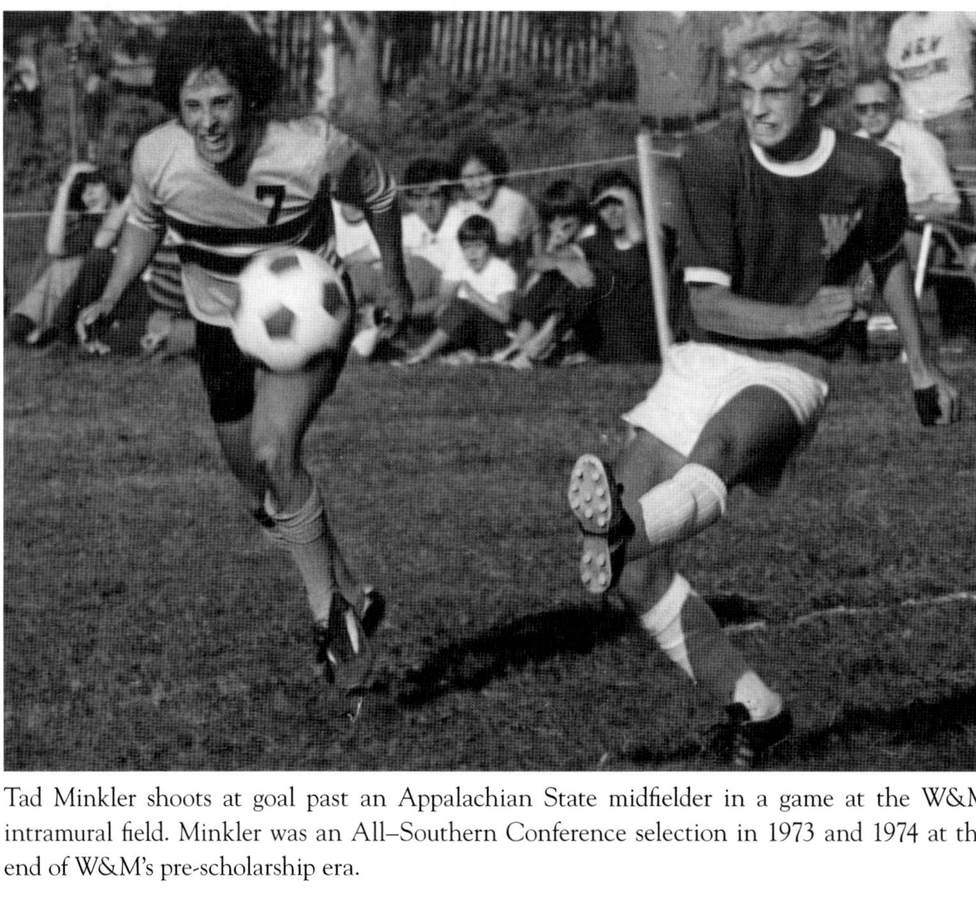

Tad Minkler shoots at goal past an Appalachian State midfielder in a game at the W&M intramural field. Minkler was an All–Southern Conference selection in 1973 and 1974 at the end of W&M's pre-scholarship era.

John McManus is still holder of the single-season goal-scoring record with 27 in the 1980 season. In the background at Cary Field is fellow Canadian and three-time All-American defender Bill Watson. McManus started the season with seven goals in the first two games and went on to establish a single-season record that has been standing for 29 years.

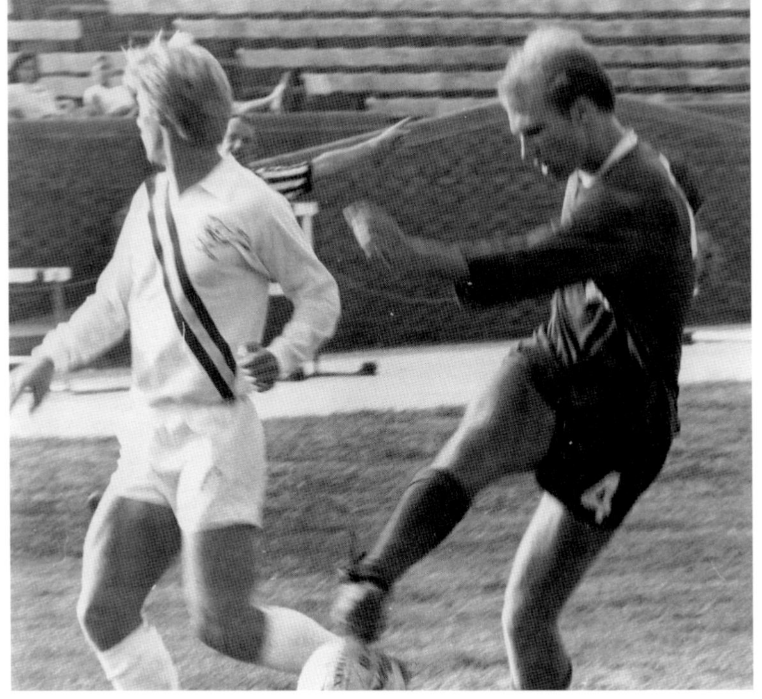

No. 4 Bill Watson pulls the ball back on an opponent at Cary Field. Watson was one of only two W&M players to be selected as All-American three times. He was the first of six outstanding Canadians to play for the Tribe between 1975 and 1987.

Billy Owens rests before a corner at the near post versus Portland in the 1994 Tribe Soccer Classic. Owens is the all-time leader in single-season assists with 16 and career assists with 41. Owens came to W&M in 1992 and helped take the program to another level. He was followed a year later by his Kempsville High School teammate, Steve Jolley, to form a very potent attacking duo.

Arguably the most dangerous player ever for the Tribe was Waughn Hughes, being rewarded here for setting the school all-time scoring record of 52 career goals. Hughes is the only player to post two 20-goal seasons. He also has the record for game-winning goals with 21. In his career, Waughn never scored more than two goals in a game, which makes his total even more impressive.

Caleb Stoddart holds the record for most matches played and started in a career, a testimony to his durability. As a freshman he started as a lone forward in a 4-5-1 system but later in his career became the lynchpin of the Tribe back four. He was an All-CAA and All–South Atlantic selection in 2000 and 2001.

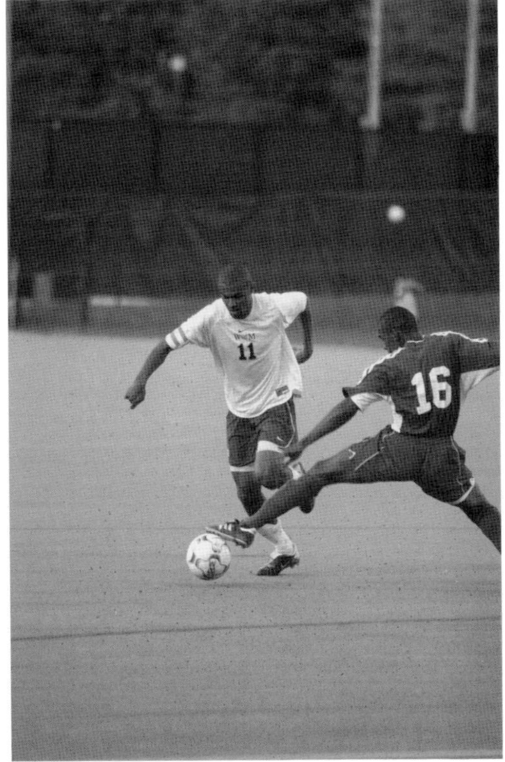

Phil Hucles, one of the most recent All-Americans from W&M, beats a defender at Busch Field. Phil came to W&M despite the fact that his sister, Angela, was a star at UVA. He stands fifth at W&M all-time in goals with 36 despite the fact that he played much of his senior year as a center back to bolster an injury-ridden Tribe defense.

Although Ricky Dahan spent just two years at W&M, he is one of only eight Tribe players to have been named an NSCAA All-American. Dahan was discovered by Coach Albert at the 1985 Maccabiah Games in Israel, when he played for the Swedish soccer team. He left school after his sophomore season to return to his club, Malmö FF.

Paul Grafer was an All-American goalkeeper for the Tribe and later played in MLS for Colorado and New York. He is in the top five in every career goalkeeping category and was W&M Male Athlete of the Year in 1995. Paul is presently a goalkeeping coach in residence with the U.S. under-17 National Team.

The team celebrates Coach Albert's 400th career win following an away game at Delaware in 2003. Albert's 401 career wins put him 11th on the all-time Division I men's soccer wins list. For coaches who have compiled all their wins at the same school, he is fourth on the all-time win list behind Jerry Yeagley of Indiana, Steve Negoesco of San Francisco, and Jack McKenzie of Quincy.

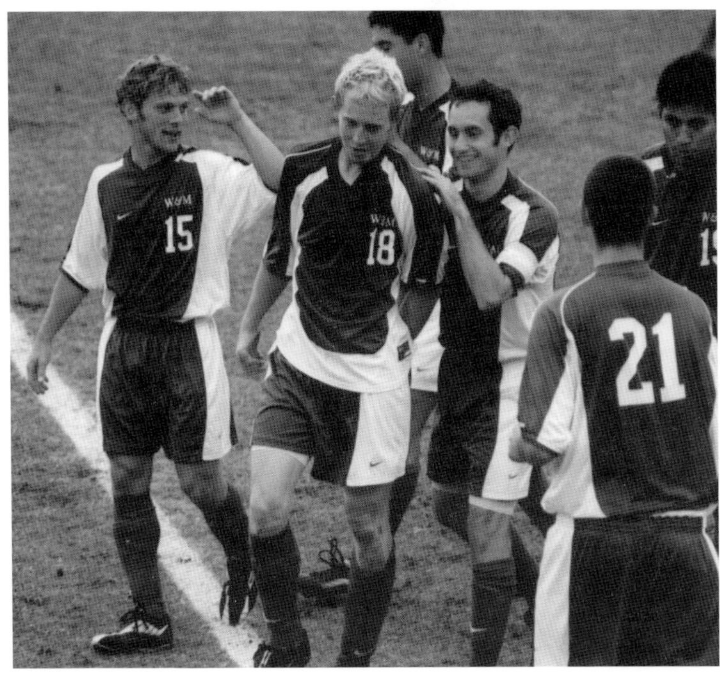

Justin Smiley was the MVP of the 2000 CAA Soccer Tournament. Smiley, who had been plagued with injuries throughout his career, had the run of his lifetime by scoring in each of the three games in the CAA tournament. He scored the game winning goal in the final versus JMU.

Jon Stewart is pictured above on W&M graduation day in 2004, looking much different than his sophomore headshot. Stewart was commencement speaker that day, and following in the footsteps of Thomas Jefferson, he received an honorary doctorate. Stewart was also honored in 2005 by the NSCAA as its Honorary All-American. Despite his fame and fortune, "Leibo" has remained the same humble person he was in 1983, as evidenced by the fact that he spent hours shaking hands and posing for pictures with literally hundreds of All-Americans at their banquet in Philadelphia in 2006.

Seven former W&M men's soccer players have been named Male Athlete of the Year at W&M. Here Scott Budnick (second from left) receives the award in 1992 from Tribe Club head Bobby Dwyer (left), athletic director John Randolph, and associate athletic director Barbara Blosser. The other recipients have been Bill Watson (1978), Mike Flood (1983), Jon Tuttle (1987), Paul Grafer (1995), Wade Barrett (1997), and Adin Brown (1999).

Only four players in the history of W&M men's soccer have scored four goals in one game. The last to do this was Ron Raab versus Christopher Newport on September 17, 1987. The other three were John McManus in 1980 versus Radford, Chris Thomas in 1975 versus Washington and Lee, and Don McCarthy in 1971 versus East Carolina. McCarthy's feat was unique in that all four goals came in the second half as the Tribe overcame a 3-0 halftime deficit to win the match 4-3. Raab is now the assistant women's soccer coach at UVA.

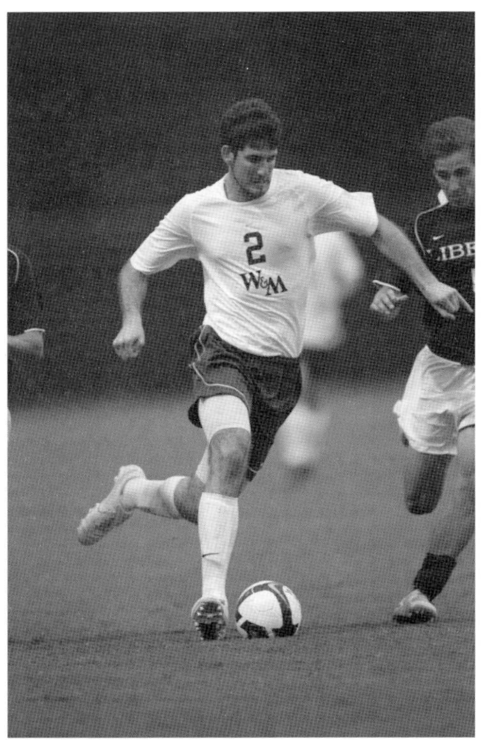

In 2009, Andrew Hoxie, a local player from the Williamsburg Soccer Club and the Virginia Legacy Soccer Club, became the only player in the history of the program to be named CAA Player of the Week four times. Here he is shown in his senior year in a preseason scrimmage against Liberty. He finished his career on the top-10 all-time career goals and points lists. In January 2010, Hoxie was chosen in the third round of the MLS draft by the San Jose Earthquakes.

Ralph Bean is not only W&M's only player from Bermuda, he is the only player in school history to play for his country in a World Cup qualifier. Bean was named Soccer News All-American in his final year in 2002, when he led the team in scoring with 11 goals and 11 assists. This was the eighth best points total by a W&M player.

9

The Spirit of Tribe Soccer

Over the door of the men's soccer locker room, a sign reads "Our Family Versus Their Team." Much goes into the development of the family spirit and tradition of W&M men's soccer, be it the annual pancake supper, the international trip every four years, or alumni weekends.

The 12th Man Club is the division of the Tribe Club that specifically supports men's soccer. Over the past 20 years, it has raised almost $1 million to support annual operating costs and also to build an endowment for men's soccer at W&M. The men's soccer endowment consists of seven separate named accounts and presently totals over $400,000.

Every four years since 1976, the Tribe soccer team has taken an international trip. The funding is always a combination of projects, such as the annual pancake supper, private donations, and contributions from the players themselves. Since the first trip to England and Holland, the team has twice visited Bermuda, Jamaica, and Greece and revisited England. The memories of these trips, usually taken in the spring, are always among the highlights of any soccer alum's experiences.

Reunion weekends are memorable also, and the team has been hosting alumni events since the early 1970s. The fall weekend now coincides with Crapolfest, an event begun to remember Andy Crapol, a former player from the local area who passed away in 2009. The weekend consists of a 5K road race event, a miniature golf tournament, and a varsity soccer match. In 2009, over 300 participants took part in the first Crapolfest weekend.

These extra events and opportunities enhance and enrich the W&M men's soccer experience, making it so much more than just four years of practices and games. As the alumni T-shirts proclaim, "Tradition Never Graduates."

The first-ever alumni game was played in the early 1970s. By 2009, the W&M alumni game attracted almost 50 former players, and the younger alumni are consistently able to give the squad a competitive game during the spring season. Shown above from left to right are (first row) Jim Wheat, Rich Atkinson, Bruce Niles, Ernie Gates, Steve Wilson, and Peter Schlief; (second row) Lyle Rosbotham, Al Albert, and Ed Hartman; (third row) Dale Mueller, Chris Gilmore, Gary King, John Burleigh, and Bob Jendron. Below is a picture from the 1979 game.

Each spring, the team conducts its annual pancake supper to raise money for the international trip it takes every four years. The Kokolis family has for years allowed W&M soccer to use its Gazebo Restaurant for the fund-raiser. Players and coaches perform all the roles in the restaurant, including cleaning, cooking, and waiting on tables. There is also an annual sale of used W&M soccer apparel. Hundreds of people are served in the three-hour event, and over a four-year period, about $10,000 is raised toward the trip. In 2003, Mike and Mario Kokolis were able to accompany the team to Athens for the eight-day tour.

This picture was taken in 1989 at the very first board meeting of the 12th Man Club, the group that raises money for men's soccer at W&M. Over the past 20 years, the group has raised over $800,000 to support the Tribe program in both annual support and endowment. The first chairman of the group was Stuart Spirn, class of 1968.

Coaches Daly and Albert pose with college president Tim Sullivan with a rendering of Albert-Daly Field. The construction of the field was made possible by a generous gift from alumni Jim and Bobbie Ukrop of Richmond. It allowed the team to move from the Astroturf facility at Busch Field to a state-of-the-art Bermuda grass field with lights and seating for 1,000 spectators.

The Tribe prepares for a game in Greece against Marcopolo, a third-division professional side. W&M has been to Athens on its last two international tours, both times hosted by the American College of Greece and its athletic director, Arthur Christopher. Besides playing several games, the Tribe has been able to visit the Parthenon and other important cultural sites. Below, the team gathers outside its bus in London at the Crystal Palace center during its 1998 England tour, during which it played six matches against professional youth and reserve teams.

On its spring trip to Bermuda in 1994, the team lines up its fleet of mopeds. This was probably not the safest way for a team to travel, but in Bermuda the options were limited. Fortunately there were no injuries except a slight case of road rash for Coach Albert. Several years later, W&M would recruit Ralph Bean, who would subsequently play for the Bermuda National Team.

This was the second trip to the island by Tribe men's soccer. This time, it was hosted by alum Charlie Franks, at that time the Young Life director in Bermuda. It was undefeated against first-division club teams. (Courtesy of Gail Albert.)

Tribe players pose with some Jamaican children after one of their games on their spring trip. The team has been twice to the island, both times staying in villas on the north coast just west of Ocho Rios near Dunns River Falls. They played a mixture of games between national league teams, such as Seba United, and local village sides. Below, a game on the coast is seen from an overlooking hill. (Both courtesy of Gail Albert.)

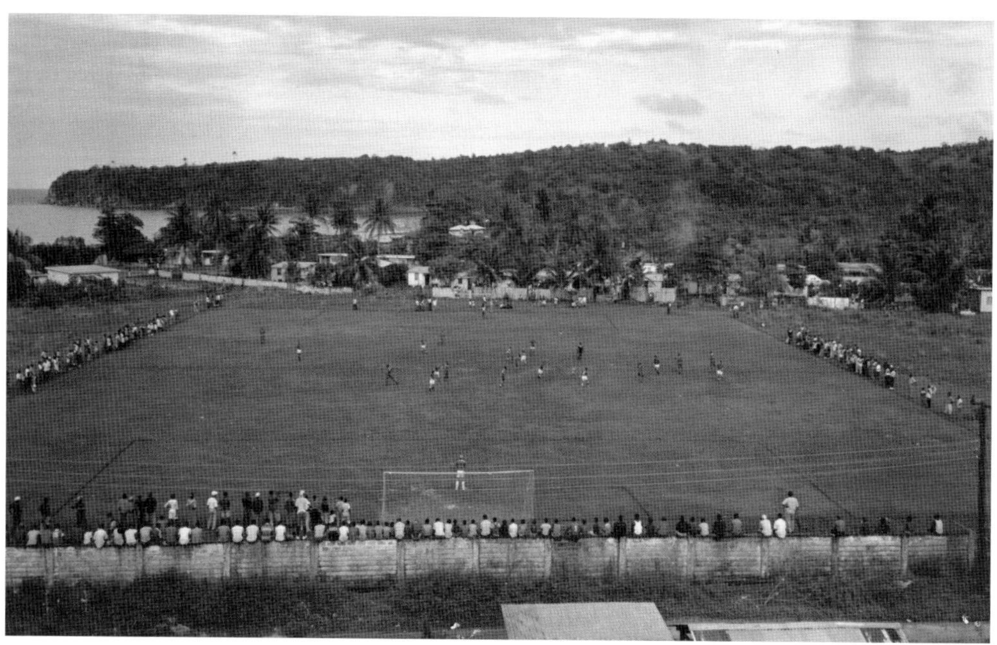

Andy Crapol was a local player from Lafayette High School and the Williamsburg Soccer Club who entered the W&M program in 1996. Although never a starter, he was an important player for team chemistry, and W&M went to the NCAA tournament all five years he was on the squad. He passed away in 2009 after a brief battle with cancer. Subsequently, a scholarship was established in his name and an annual fall event called Crapolfest, which coincides with the fall soccer reunion weekend, creates revenue for the fund. As part of Crapolfest, the team helps conduct a 5K race and also a miniature golf outing.

Tribe soccer has played twice in the University of Portland fall soccer tournament. Given that Nike has been the longtime sponsor of the W&M program, this has been an opportunity for the team to visit the Nike New World Campus in Beaverton. Here the players pose for a team shot with the statue of Ronaldo at the soccer field on campus.

Brannon Thomas was the winner of the CAA's John Randolph Inspiration Award in 2004. "Z" underwent surgery for a brain tumor over the summer of 2003 and returned to action the last two games of the season. In 2004, he headed home the winning goal in a 1-0 upset of number-one-ranked Maryland at Albert-Daly Field. His younger brother Caleb is now a midfielder for the Tribe.

In 2004, W&M soccer moved into its new home, hopefully the last stop in a journey that has taken the team from the college's intramural field to James Blair Terrace to Cary Field to Busch Field and now finally back to the Dillard Complex (formerly JBT). Plans are being developed to add the necessary amenities of bathrooms, locker rooms, press boxes, concessions, and so on, but the playing surface and lights are top-notch. In 2008, the NCAA playoffs finally returned to Williamsburg, and hopefully, there will be many more opportunities in the future for men's and women's soccer to host postseason matches.

Halftime receptions have become a regular event at men's and women's games, sponsored by the 12th Man Club and the Friends of Women's Soccer. Eventually the new stadium will have an area built to accommodate the ever-growing crowd of supporters.

In 2009, on the 25th anniversary of his graduation from W&M, an anonymous donor created the Neil Sherman Soccer Scholarship. Sherman was a member of the team from 1979 to 1982. Although never a starter for the Tribe, Sherman loved the game and continued to play until his untimely passing in 2001. The scholarship will be awarded annually to a member of the team who, like Sherman, has an artistic or musical talent.

Josh Quinter was a two-year captain for the Tribe in 1996 and 1997. After seeing limited action in seven games as a freshman, Quinter moved into a starting role his sophomore year. In 1995, he scored five goals from a defensive position and was named Most Improved. His leadership was a key factor in the team's success from 1995 to 1997. After graduation, Quinter attended law school at Villanova and has practiced law in Philadelphia since earning his degree and passing the Pennsylvania Bar. He recently declared his candidacy for the 13th District U.S. Congressional seat. He could become the first former Tribe soccer player in the U.S. House of Representatives.

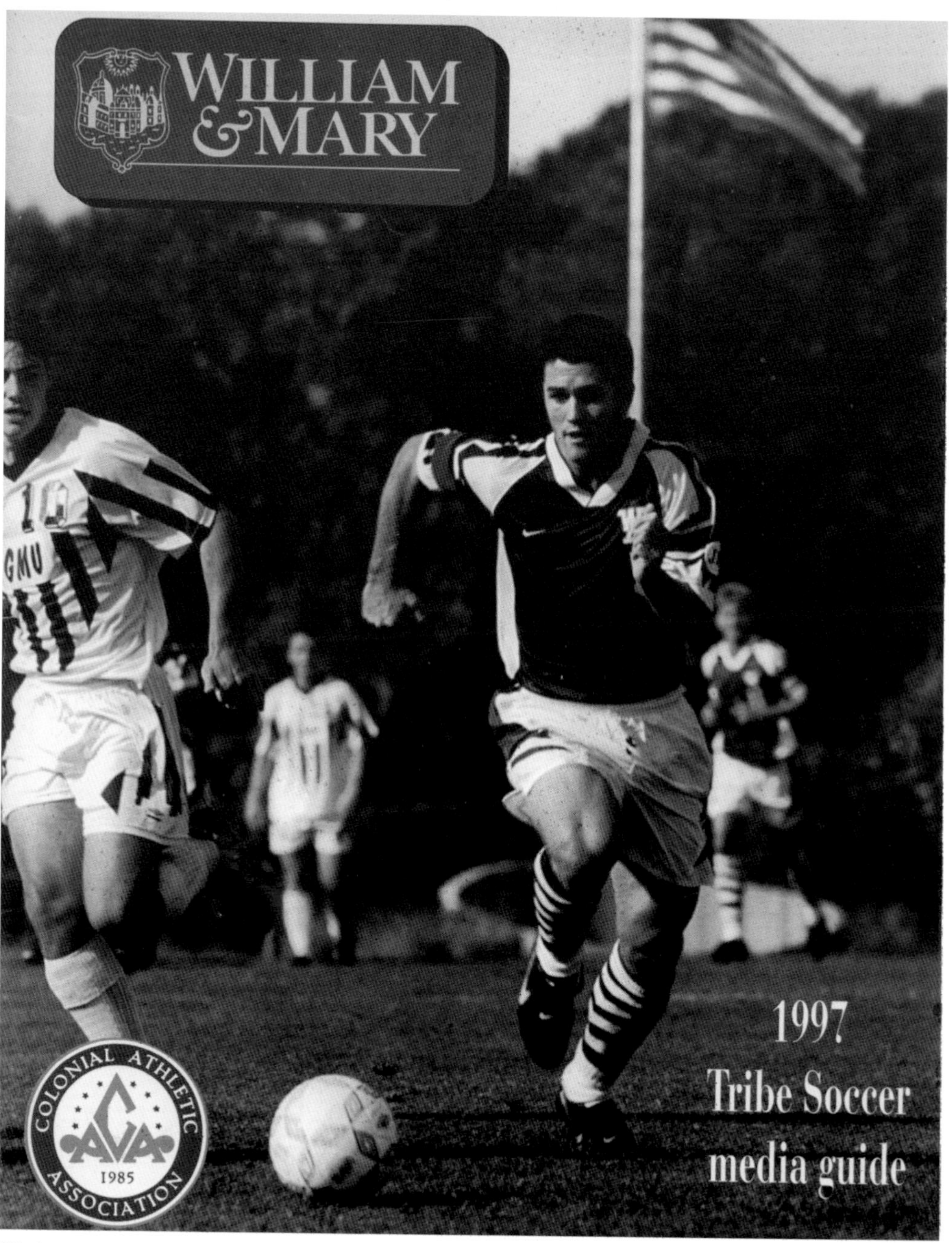

Wade Barrett, pictured here on the cover of the 1997 media guide, was a four-year starter for the Tribe. He finished his career in the top 10 of every offensive category. A talented athlete, Wade could win the shuttle run, the 50-yard dash, and the 2-mile run in team fitness competition. His greatest assets, and that which have taken him to become the captain of an MLS championship team, are his competitiveness and great team spirit. Even as a senior, he would be the first to pitch in and pick up the cones or collect the balls at the end of practice. Wade was an All-American in 1997 and CAA Player of the Year. He was also a four-time All-CAA first-team selection.

L

LETTERMEN

Nick Abrigo	2008–09	Adin Brown * # †	1996–99	Paul Cushman	1969
Bob Ageloff	1981–84	Alex Brown	2000–03	Jano Cymes	1977
John Ahearn	1976	Clement Brown	1970–71	Ricky Dahan * # †	1986–87
Al Albert	1966, 68	Rob Bryden	1994–96	Mike Darr	1967
Graham Albert * #	2000–03	Derek Buckley	2007–09	Chris Darton	1971
Doug Allman	1976	Scott Budnick * #	1989–92	Tom Daskaloff	1974
John Allman	1970–73	Chris Burgess	1999–02	Chris Davin #	1976–79
Tarek Amyuni	1983	John Burleigh	1966–69	Kirk Day	1989
Ben Anderson	2009	Martin Burroughs	1965	Rick Derflinger	1979–82
Brad Anger	1991	Greg Butler	1990–91	Ridge DeWitt	1972–75
Doug Annakin	1984–87	Joe Carlin	1974–77	Don Dichiara	1984–87
Mike Atienza	1992	Dan Carrigan	1967	Larry Dillion	1965–66
Rich Atkinson	1968–70	Jimmy Carroll	2008–09	Michael DiNuzzo	2007–09
George Attoh	1977–78	Guy Cartwright	1990–93	Boro Djordjevic	1970–72
Nathaniel Baako *#	2007–09	Jonas Cedergren	1985–88	John Dodds	1967–70
Todd Bachman	1991–92	Andy Chapin	1991–93	Jeff Dominquez	1995–98
Glenn Balas	1975	Garrett Chittum	1996–99	Chris Drescher	1989–92
Wade Barrett * # †	1994–97	Steve Christie	1987	Gary Duggan	1970–72
Hart Baur	1982–85	Peter Christmas	2007–09	Eric Dumbleton *	1989–92
Ralph Bean * #	1999–02	John Chuday	1978–80	Joe Dunbeck	1971–72
Allen Beasley	1972–74	Brian Clarke	1965	Gordon Eide	1972
Matt Becker	2009	Pete Clarke	1965	Bill Eisner	1984–85
Tim Becker	2009	Bob Claude	1971	David Eklund	1978–79
Mike Bedell	1978–81	Bruce Cleland	1971–72	David Ellenbogen	1975–78
Nathan Belcher	2006–08	Michael Clemons	1987	Bruce Ensley	1986–89
Scott Bell * #	1983–86	Chris Clifford	1973–74	Tom Erdman	1981–83
Bruce Bender *	1976–77	John Coffin	1994–98	Doug Ernst	2004–07
Larry Berbert	1976–77	Art Cone	1971–72	Bo Eskay	1986–87
Mike Berbert	1970–72	Derek Connell	1984	Phil Essman	1969–70
Paul Berge	1967–68	John Corbett	1967	Brad Eure	1975–78
Paul Bjarnason	1986–89	Joseph Cosimano	1971–72	Keith Exton	1981–84
Bob Boal	1966–67	Peter Coughter	2001–02	Dave Fabian #	1967–70
Luke Bocklemann	1995–98	Andy Crapol	1997–2000	Conor Farley	1985–88
Roger Bothe *	2006–09	Bill Crewe	1965–66	Chris Felder	1973
Michael Botta *	1993–96	Larry Crisman	1983	Robin Felder	1973
Todd Bromfeld	1973–75	Joe Crowley	1979–80	John Feldmann	1997, 99–2000
Martin Brady	2004–05	Paul Crowley	1980	Kris Feldmann	2000–03
John Bray	1976–79	Mike Cummings	1987–91	George Fenigsohn	1966–67
Keith Bricklemeyer	1966–67	Darcy Curran	1983–86	Jeff Finnegan	1967–68

Gerald Fitzpatrick 1972–73
Dan Flaherty 1995–98
Mike Flood # † 1980–83
Alan Forde 1968
James Fox * 1972–75
Larry Fox 1966
Dave Francombe 1988
Steve Gallop 1977–80
Carlos F. Garcia # * 1999–2002
Mark Gardiner # 1977, 79–81
Steve Gaskins 1965–66, 68
Ernie Gates 1968–69
Duane Gerenser 1967
Kip Germain * # 1975–78
Ali Ghassemi * 1986–90
Chris Gilmore 1968, 71
Ben Glass 1976–79
Rob Godwin 2006–07
Mark Goldberg 1982–83
Alan Golden 1999–2002
Andy Goldsmith 1979
Chris Goodwin 1971
Paul Grafer * # † 1992–95
Steve Graine # 1979–82
Lee Graves 1968
Jeff Greim 1970–73
Summers Hambrick 1983, 85–87
Matt Hansen 1996–99
Jeremy Harris 2006–09
Ed Hartman 1967–70
Jim Hauschild * # 1988–91
Mike Hause 1972–74
Mark Healy * 1972–74
Al Heck 1976–78
Bob Hennessey 1977
Doug Henry 1999–2002
Charles Hensel * 1974–77
Miguel Hernandez 1997–2001
Stu Hilder 1965
Brian Hinkey * # 1997–99
Bryan Hinkle * 2001–04
Adam Hogge 1982–85
Lance Holland 1983–86
Steve Holmes 1971
Andrew Hoxie * # 2005–06, 08–09
Phil Hucles * # † 2000–03
Stephen Hughes 2003–04
Waughn Hughes * # † 1993–96
Bob Jendron 1967–70
Steve Jolley * # 1993–96
Brock Jones * 2005–07
Mike Jones 1980–82
Mike Kalaris 1982–85
Peter Kalaris 1978–81
Jon Kamara 1989–92
Tim Kassel 2000–02
Jason Katner 1986–89
Scott Kelsey 2003–06
Richard Kent 1973
Tim Kilgore 1994
John Kim 1971
Mike King-Harmon 1965–66
Gary King * 1965–66
Kip Kintzer 1973
Ed Klein 1967
Juergen Kloo 1979–82
Kevin Knott * # + 1997–2000
Alan Koger 2007–09
Steve Kokulis * # 1986–89
Ron Kraemer 1978–80
Greg Lalas 1990
David Lam 1979–82
Steve Lancashire 1966–69
Tim Larkin 1984–87
Steve Lawrence 1968
Stephen Laws 2008–09
John Lee 2004–05
Jon Leibowitz 1981–83
Bernard Leister 1972
Joel Lewin 1986–88
Heldur Liivak 1971–74
Ky Lindsey 1976
Glenn Livingstone 1982–85
James Lofton 2009
Eduardo Lopez * # 1976–77
Art Louise 1965–66
Scott MacLaren # 1972–74
Bob Mageras 1983
Andrew Mahan 2008–09
Chris Maher 1975–77, 79
Jeff Marklin 2003–06
Cameron Mayer 1997–99
Andrew McAdams 2007–09
Doug McBride * 2005–08
Desmond McCarthy 1994–96
Don McCarthy 1970–71
Kieran McCarthy * 1988–91
Brendan McCurdy 2003–06
Scott McEvoy 1967–70
Joe McGovern 1991–94
Tom McGovern 1970–71
David McGowan * 1994–97
John McManus # 1978–80
Scott Meardon 1973
John Metzger 1989–91, 93
Stu Meyerson 1967
Todd Middlebrook * 1981–84
B.A. Miller 1970
Richard Miller 1980–83
Tad Minkler * 1973-76
Rich Miranda * # 1981–82, 84–85
Drew Misher 1989
John Mohseni 1991–94
Dale Mueller 1965–67
Brian Mullins 1978
Pat Murcia 1987–88
Craig Myers 2002–05
Marty Nickley 1977–80
Bruce Niles 1967–70
Chris Norris * # 1991–94
Andreas Nydal 2002–05
Randy Oakes 1980
Dave Oelberg 1970–72
Pat O'Hara 1971
John Olsen 1970–73
Rob Olson # 1977–80
Nicholas Orozco 2007–09
Ryan Overdevest + 2004–07
Billy Owens * # 1992–95
Bob Owens 1982
Matt Pagels 1967
Gates Parker 1971–72
Kevin Parks 1976–79
Chris Perez 2009
Ed Perry 1984–85
Ian Peter * 1984–87
Andrew Petty 1992–95
Don Pfanz 1976–77
Andrew Pillari 1997–2000
Billy Platz 1998–2001
Joe Pombriant 1994–96
Christian Powers 1989–92

Scott Powers	1994–96
Curtis Pride	1987
Tim Prisco	1992–93
Steve Proscino *	1972–74
Josh Quinter *	1994–97
Ron Raab	1985–88
Nick Radkowsky	1998
Kris Rake	2003–06
Chris Raney	1974
John Rasnic	1979, 81–83
Mike Repke	1987
Scott Repke	1982–85
Tom Repke	1984
Brian Reshefsky	1992–94
Doug Reynolds	1971
Rick Rheinhardt	1972–73
Shawn Rice	1996, 98–99
Greg Richards	1992–95
Wayne Richardson	1968
Scott Ritter	1994–95
Chris Rodd *	2003–04
Lyle Rosbotham	1968
Andrew Ross	1998–2001
Steve Row	1965–66
Rich Ruhr	1982
Lucas Salcedo	2000–03
Mark Sartor	1978–79
Chris Sartorius	1980–81
Scott Satterfield	1972–75
Dave Schaefer	1978–79
Pat Scherder * #	2002–06
David Schifrin	1992–95
Pete Schleif	1966–68
Adam Schultz	1997–2000
Chris Scrofani*	1992–95
Ryan Sells	2004–07
Dan Sheehan	1983–84
Neil Sherman	1979–80, 82
Dee Sibley	1968
Storm Simenson	1975–76
Phil Simonpietri	1974–76
John Siner	1988–91
William A. Singleton	1965
Justin Smiley	1999–2002
Charles Smith	1981, 1983
Maurice Smith	1988–91
Rick Smith	1974–76
Trevor Smith *	1972–75
Andy Smolin	1981–84
Colin Smolinsky	2008–09
Dave Snyder	1981–83
Ryan Snyder	2008–09
Geoff Solomon	1984
Joe Soos	1992–95
Rich Spencer	1985–88
Stu Spirn	1966
Tim Stamps	1969–72
Dave Starks	1988–91
John Sterrett	1971–72
Val Stieglitz	1970
Khary Stockton *	1989–92
Caleb Stoddart * #	1998–2001
Ian Stowe	2007–09
George Strong	1987–90
Thom Sutlive	1980–83
Vins Sutlive	1973–76
Graham Sykes * #	1976–79
Steve Szczypinski	1986–89
Mark Taylor	1967–68, 70
Martin Taylor	1985–88
Guy Temple	1965
Andrew Terry	2001–04
Brannon Thomas *	2000–04
Caleb Thomas	2009
Chris Thomas	1974–75
Jarrett Thomas	2003–06
Price Thomas *	2006–09
Richard Tillberg	1965
Spencer Timm	1965–66
Casey Todd * #	1973–75
Scott Tretheway	1984
Mulumba Tshishimbi	1992–95
Eric Tullio	1977, 1979
Greg Turk	1989–92
Jon Tuttle * # +	1985–88
Bob Tuttle	1981
Trevor Upton	1999–2002
Gabe Valencia	1996
Larry Valentine	1986–89
Joel Vecere	1998–2001
Dave Viscovich *	1988–91
Clayton Voss	2002–05
Terry Vought	1968–69
Nelson Warley	1994–97
Andy Watson #	1983
Bill Watson * # †	1975–78
Steven Way	1970–71
Chris Wayne	2004–06
Brennan Wergley	2004–07
Greg Westfall	1993, 96–97
Brian White	1974
Tom Wieboldt	1967
Preston Whitlock	2006–09
Scott Williams	1988–91
Steve Wilson	1967–70
Paul Wise	1979–80
David Wong	1985
Richard Wong	1984–85
Mike Wren	1970
Michael Yakovac	2004–07
Mike Yap	1971
Colin Young	2001–04
Jason Zawacki	1992
Dan Zickefoose	1994–97
Nimrod Zosim * #	1991
Mike Zwicklbauer	1981–83

* All-conference selection
# All-region selection
† All-America selection
\+ Academic All-America selection

Please notify the William and Mary sports information office with corrections or additions to this list.

www.arcadiapublishing.com

Discover books about the town where you grew up, the cities where your friends and families live, the town where your parents met, or even that retirement spot you've been dreaming about. Our Web site provides history lovers with exclusive deals, advanced notification about new titles, e-mail alerts of author events, and much more.

Arcadia Publishing, the leading local history publisher in the United States, is committed to making history accessible and meaningful through publishing books that celebrate and preserve the heritage of America's people and places. Consistent with our mission to preserve history on a local level, this book was printed in South Carolina on American-made paper and manufactured entirely in the United States.

This book carries the accredited Forest Stewardship Council (FSC) label and is printed on 100 percent FSC-certified paper. Products carrying the FSC label are independently certified to assure consumers that they come from forests that are managed to meet the social, economic, and ecological needs of present and future generations.

Cert no. SW-COC-001530
www.fsc.org
© 1996 Forest Stewardship Council

Find *Your* Place in History.